WEST-E
Middle Level Humanities (052/053)

SECRETS

Study Guide
Your Key to Exam Success

WEST-E Test Review for the
Washington Educator Skills
Tests-Endorsements

Dear Future Exam Success Story:

First of all, **THANK YOU** for purchasing Mometrix study materials!

Second, congratulations! You are one of the few determined test-takers who are committed to doing whatever it takes to excel on your exam. **You have come to the right place.** We developed these study materials with one goal in mind: to deliver you the information you need in a format that's concise and easy to use.

In addition to optimizing your guide for the content of the test, we've outlined our recommended steps for breaking down the preparation process into small, attainable goals so you can make sure you stay on track.

We've also analyzed the entire test-taking process, identifying the most common pitfalls and showing how you can overcome them and be ready for any curveball the test throws you.

Standardized testing is one of the biggest obstacles on your road to success, which only increases the importance of doing well in the high-pressure, high-stakes environment of test day. Your results on this test could have a significant impact on your future, and this guide provides the information and practical advice to help you achieve your full potential on test day.

Your success is our success

We would love to hear from you! If you would like to share the story of your exam success or if you have any questions or comments in regard to our products, please contact us at **800-673-8175** or **support@mometrix.com**.

Thanks again for your business and we wish you continued success!

Sincerely,
The Mometrix Test Preparation Team

Need more help? Check out our flashcards at: <u>http://mometrixflashcards.com/WEST</u>

TABLE OF CONTENTS

Introduction

Thank you for purchasing this resource! You have made the choice to prepare yourself for a test that could have a huge impact on your future, and this guide is designed to help you be fully ready for test day. Obviously, it's important to have a solid understanding of the test material, but you also need to be prepared for the unique environment and stressors of the test, so that you can perform to the best of your abilities.

For this purpose, the first section that appears in this guide is the **Secret Keys**. We've devoted countless hours to meticulously researching what works and what doesn't, and we've boiled down our findings to the five most impactful steps you can take to improve your performance on the test. We start at the beginning with study planning and move through the preparation process, all the way to the testing strategies that will help you get the most out of what you know when you're finally sitting in front of the test.

We recommend that you start preparing for your test as far in advance as possible. However, if you've bought this guide as a last-minute study resource and only have a few days before your test, we recommend that you skip over the first two Secret Keys since they address a long-term study plan.

If you struggle with **test anxiety**, we strongly encourage you to check out our recommendations for how you can overcome it. Test anxiety is a formidable foe, but it can be beaten, and we want to make sure you have the tools you need to defeat it.

Secret Key #1 – Plan Big, Study Small

There's a lot riding on your performance. If you want to ace this test, you're going to need to keep your skills sharp and the material fresh in your mind. You need a plan that lets you review everything you need to know while still fitting in your schedule. We'll break this strategy down into three categories.

Information Organization

Start with the information you already have: the official test outline. From this, you can make a complete list of all the concepts you need to cover before the test. Organize these concepts into groups that can be studied together, and create a list of any related vocabulary you need to learn so you can brush up on any difficult terms. You'll want to keep this vocabulary list handy once you actually start studying since you may need to add to it along the way.

Time Management

Once you have your set of study concepts, decide how to spread them out over the time you have left before the test. Break your study plan into small, clear goals so you have a manageable task for each day and know exactly what you're doing. Then just focus on one small step at a time. When you manage your time this way, you don't need to spend hours at a time studying. Studying a small block of content for a short period each day helps you retain information better and avoid stressing over how much you have left to do. You can relax knowing that you have a plan to cover everything in time. In order for this strategy to be effective though, you have to start studying early and stick to your schedule. Avoid the exhaustion and futility that comes from last-minute cramming!

Study Environment

The environment you study in has a big impact on your learning. Studying in a coffee shop, while probably more enjoyable, is not likely to be as fruitful as studying in a quiet room. It's important to keep distractions to a minimum. You're only planning to study for a short block of time, so make the most of it. Don't pause to check your phone or get up to find a snack. It's also important to **avoid multitasking**. Research has consistently shown that multitasking will make your studying dramatically less effective. Your study area should also be comfortable and well-lit so you don't have the distraction of straining your eyes or sitting on an uncomfortable chair.

The time of day you study is also important. You want to be rested and alert. Don't wait until just before bedtime. Study when you'll be most likely to comprehend and remember. Even better, if you know what time of day your test will be, set that time aside for study. That way your brain will be used to working on that subject at that specific time and you'll have a better chance of recalling information.

Finally, it can be helpful to team up with others who are studying for the same test. Your actual studying should be done in as isolated an environment as possible, but the work of organizing the information and setting up the study plan can be divided up. In between study sessions, you can discuss with your teammates the concepts that you're all studying and quiz each other on the details. Just be sure that your teammates are as serious about the test as you are. If you find that your study time is being replaced with social time, you might need to find a new team.

Secret Key #2 – Make Your Studying Count

You're devoting a lot of time and effort to preparing for this test, so you want to be absolutely certain it will pay off. This means doing more than just reading the content and hoping you can remember it on test day. It's important to make every minute of study count. There are two main areas you can focus on to make your studying count:

Retention

It doesn't matter how much time you study if you can't remember the material. You need to make sure you are retaining the concepts. To check your retention of the information you're learning, try recalling it at later times with minimal prompting. Try carrying around flashcards and glance at one or two from time to time or ask a friend who's also studying for the test to quiz you.

To enhance your retention, look for ways to put the information into practice so that you can apply it rather than simply recalling it. If you're using the information in practical ways, it will be much easier to remember. Similarly, it helps to solidify a concept in your mind if you're not only reading it to yourself but also explaining it to someone else. Ask a friend to let you teach them about a concept you're a little shaky on (or speak aloud to an imaginary audience if necessary). As you try to summarize, define, give examples, and answer your friend's questions, you'll understand the concepts better and they will stay with you longer. Finally, step back for a big picture view and ask yourself how each piece of information fits with the whole subject. When you link the different concepts together and see them working together as a whole, it's easier to remember the individual components.

Finally, practice showing your work on any multi-step problems, even if you're just studying. Writing out each step you take to solve a problem will help solidify the process in your mind, and you'll be more likely to remember it during the test.

Modality

Modality simply refers to the means or method by which you study. Choosing a study modality that fits your own individual learning style is crucial. No two people learn best in exactly the same way, so it's important to know your strengths and use them to your advantage.

For example, if you learn best by visualization, focus on visualizing a concept in your mind and draw an image or a diagram. Try color-coding your notes, illustrating them, or creating symbols that will trigger your mind to recall a learned concept. If you learn best by hearing or discussing information, find a study partner who learns the same way or read aloud to yourself. Think about how to put the information in your own words. Imagine that you are giving a lecture on the topic and record yourself so you can listen to it later.

For any learning style, flashcards can be helpful. Organize the information so you can take advantage of spare moments to review. Underline key words or phrases. Use different colors for different categories. Mnemonic devices (such as creating a short list in which every item starts with the same letter) can also help with retention. Find what works best for you and use it to store the information in your mind most effectively and easily.

Secret Key #3 – Practice the Right Way

Your success on test day depends not only on how many hours you put into preparing, but also on whether you prepared the right way. It's good to check along the way to see if your studying is paying off. One of the most effective ways to do this is by taking practice tests to evaluate your progress. Practice tests are useful because they show exactly where you need to improve. Every time you take a practice test, pay special attention to these three groups of questions:

- The questions you got wrong
- The questions you had to guess on, even if you guessed right
- The questions you found difficult or slow to work through

This will show you exactly what your weak areas are, and where you need to devote more study time. Ask yourself why each of these questions gave you trouble. Was it because you didn't understand the material? Was it because you didn't remember the vocabulary? Do you need more repetitions on this type of question to build speed and confidence? Dig into those questions and figure out how you can strengthen your weak areas as you go back to review the material.

Additionally, many practice tests have a section explaining the answer choices. It can be tempting to read the explanation and think that you now have a good understanding of the concept. However, an explanation likely only covers part of the question's broader context. Even if the explanation makes sense, **go back and investigate** every concept related to the question until you're positive you have a thorough understanding.

As you go along, keep in mind that the practice test is just that: practice. Memorizing these questions and answers will not be very helpful on the actual test because it is unlikely to have any of the same exact questions. If you only know the right answers to the sample questions, you won't be prepared for the real thing. **Study the concepts** until you understand them fully, and then you'll be able to answer any question that shows up on the test.

It's important to wait on the practice tests until you're ready. If you take a test on your first day of study, you may be overwhelmed by the amount of material covered and how much you need to learn. Work up to it gradually.

On test day, you'll need to be prepared for answering questions, managing your time, and using the test-taking strategies you've learned. It's a lot to balance, like a mental marathon that will have a big impact on your future. Like training for a marathon, you'll need to start slowly and work your way up. When test day arrives, you'll be ready.

Start with the strategies you've read in the first two Secret Keys—plan your course and study in the way that works best for you. If you have time, consider using multiple study resources to get different approaches to the same concepts. It can be helpful to see difficult concepts from more than one angle. Then find a good source for practice tests. Many times, the test website will suggest potential study resources or provide sample tests.

Practice Test Strategy

When you're ready to start taking practice tests, follow this strategy:

Untimed and Open-Book Practice

Take the first test with no time constraints and with your notes and study guide handy. Take your time and focus on applying the strategies you've learned.

Timed and Open-Book Practice

Take the second practice test open-book as well, but set a timer and practice pacing yourself to finish in time.

Timed and Closed-Book Practice

Take any other practice tests as if it were test day. Set a timer and put away your study materials. Sit at a table or desk in a quiet room, imagine yourself at the testing center, and answer questions as quickly and accurately as possible.

Keep repeating timed and closed-book tests on a regular basis until you run out of practice tests or it's time for the actual test. Your mind will be ready for the schedule and stress of test day, and you'll be able to focus on recalling the material you've learned.

Secret Key #4 – Pace Yourself

Once you're fully prepared for the material on the test, your biggest challenge on test day will be managing your time. Just knowing that the clock is ticking can make you panic even if you have plenty of time left. Work on pacing yourself so you can build confidence against the time constraints of the exam. Pacing is a difficult skill to master, especially in a high-pressure environment, so **practice is vital**.

Set time expectations for your pace based on how much time is available. For example, if a section has 60 questions and the time limit is 30 minutes, you know you have to average 30 seconds or less per question in order to answer them all. Although 30 seconds is the hard limit, set 25 seconds per question as your goal, so you reserve extra time to spend on harder questions. When you budget extra time for the harder questions, you no longer have any reason to stress when those questions take longer to answer.

Don't let this time expectation distract you from working through the test at a calm, steady pace, but keep it in mind so you don't spend too much time on any one question. Recognize that taking extra time on one question you don't understand may keep you from answering two that you do understand later in the test. If your time limit for a question is up and you're still not sure of the answer, mark it and move on, and come back to it later if the time and the test format allow. If the testing format doesn't allow you to return to earlier questions, just make an educated guess; then put it out of your mind and move on.

On the easier questions, be careful not to rush. It may seem wise to hurry through them so you have more time for the challenging ones, but it's not worth missing one if you know the concept and just didn't take the time to read the question fully. Work efficiently but make sure you understand the question and have looked at all of the answer choices, since more than one may seem right at first.

Even if you're paying attention to the time, you may find yourself a little behind at some point. You should speed up to get back on track, but do so wisely. Don't panic; just take a few seconds less on each question until you're caught up. Don't guess without thinking, but do look through the answer choices and eliminate any you know are wrong. If you can get down to two choices, it is often worthwhile to guess from those. Once you've chosen an answer, move on and don't dwell on any that you skipped or had to hurry through. If a question was taking too long, chances are it was one of the harder ones, so you weren't as likely to get it right anyway.

On the other hand, if you find yourself getting ahead of schedule, it may be beneficial to slow down a little. The more quickly you work, the more likely you are to make a careless mistake that will affect your score. You've budgeted time for each question, so don't be afraid to spend that time. Practice an efficient but careful pace to get the most out of the time you have.

Secret Key #5 – Have a Plan for Guessing

When you're taking the test, you may find yourself stuck on a question. Some of the answer choices seem better than others, but you don't see the one answer choice that is obviously correct. What do you do?

The scenario described above is very common, yet most test takers have not effectively prepared for it. Developing and practicing a plan for guessing may be one of the single most effective uses of your time as you get ready for the exam.

In developing your plan for guessing, there are three questions to address:

- When should you start the guessing process?
- How should you narrow down the choices?
- Which answer should you choose?

When to Start the Guessing Process

Unless your plan for guessing is to select C every time (which, despite its merits, is not what we recommend), you need to leave yourself enough time to apply your answer elimination strategies. Since you have a limited amount of time for each question, that means that if you're going to give yourself the best shot at guessing correctly, you have to decide quickly whether or not you will guess.

Of course, the best-case scenario is that you don't have to guess at all, so first, see if you can answer the question based on your knowledge of the subject and basic reasoning skills. Focus on the key words in the question and try to jog your memory of related topics. Give yourself a chance to bring the knowledge to mind, but once you realize that you don't have (or you can't access) the knowledge you need to answer the question, it's time to start the guessing process.

It's almost always better to start the guessing process too early than too late. It only takes a few seconds to remember something and answer the question from knowledge. Carefully eliminating wrong answer choices takes longer. Plus, going through the process of eliminating answer choices can actually help jog your memory.

Summary: Start the guessing process as soon as you decide that you can't answer the question based on your knowledge.

How to Narrow Down the Choices

The next chapter in this book (**Test-Taking Strategies**) includes a wide range of strategies for how to approach questions and how to look for answer choices to eliminate. You will definitely want to read those carefully, practice them, and figure out which ones work best for you. Here though, we're going to address a mindset rather than a particular strategy.

Your chances of guessing an answer correctly depend on how many options you are choosing from.

How many choices you have	How likely you are to guess correctly
5	20%
4	25%
3	33%
2	50%
1	100%

You can see from this chart just how valuable it is to be able to eliminate incorrect answers and make an educated guess, but there are two things that many test takers do that cause them to miss out on the benefits of guessing:

- Accidentally eliminating the correct answer
- Selecting an answer based on an impression

We'll look at the first one here, and the second one in the next section.

To avoid accidentally eliminating the correct answer, we recommend a thought exercise called **the $5 challenge**. In this challenge, you only eliminate an answer choice from contention if you are willing to bet $5 on it being wrong. Why $5? Five dollars is a small but not insignificant amount of money. It's an amount you could afford to lose but wouldn't want to throw away. And while losing $5 once might not hurt too much, doing it twenty times will set you back $100. In the same way, each small decision you make—eliminating a choice here, guessing on a question there—won't by itself impact your score very much, but when you put them all together, they can make a big difference. By holding each answer choice elimination decision to a higher standard, you can reduce the risk of accidentally eliminating the correct answer.

The $5 challenge can also be applied in a positive sense: If you are willing to bet $5 that an answer choice *is* correct, go ahead and mark it as correct.

Summary: Only eliminate an answer choice if you are willing to bet $5 that it is wrong.

Which Answer to Choose

You're taking the test. You've run into a hard question and decided you'll have to guess. You've eliminated all the answer choices you're willing to bet $5 on. Now you have to pick an answer. Why do we even need to talk about this? Why can't you just pick whichever one you feel like when the time comes?

The answer to these questions is that if you don't come into the test with a plan, you'll rely on your impression to select an answer choice, and if you do that, you risk falling into a trap. The test writers know that everyone who takes their test will be guessing on some of the questions, so they intentionally write wrong answer choices to seem plausible. You still have to pick an answer though, and if the wrong answer choices are designed to look right, how can you ever be sure that you're not falling for their trap? The best solution we've found to this dilemma is to take the decision out of your hands entirely. Here is the process we recommend:

Once you've eliminated any choices that you are confident (willing to bet $5) are wrong, select the first remaining choice as your answer.

Whether you choose to select the first remaining choice, the second, or the last, the important thing is that you use some preselected standard. Using this approach guarantees that you will not be enticed into selecting an answer choice that looks right, because you are not basing your decision on how the answer choices look.

This is not meant to make you question your knowledge. Instead, it is to help you recognize the difference between your knowledge and your impressions. There's a huge difference between thinking an answer is right because of what you know, and thinking an answer is right because it looks or sounds like it should be right.

Summary: To ensure that your selection is appropriately random, make a predetermined selection from among all answer choices you have not eliminated.

Test-Taking Strategies

This section contains a list of test-taking strategies that you may find helpful as you work through the test. By taking what you know and applying logical thought, you can maximize your chances of answering any question correctly!

It is very important to realize that every question is different and every person is different: no single strategy will work on every question, and no single strategy will work for every person. That's why we've included all of them here, so you can try them out and determine which ones work best for different types of questions and which ones work best for you.

Question Strategies

Read Carefully

Read the question and answer choices carefully. Don't miss the question because you misread the terms. You have plenty of time to read each question thoroughly and make sure you understand what is being asked. Yet a happy medium must be attained, so don't waste too much time. You must read carefully, but efficiently.

Contextual Clues

Look for contextual clues. If the question includes a word you are not familiar with, look at the immediate context for some indication of what the word might mean. Contextual clues can often give you all the information you need to decipher the meaning of an unfamiliar word. Even if you can't determine the meaning, you may be able to narrow down the possibilities enough to make a solid guess at the answer to the question.

Prefixes

If you're having trouble with a word in the question or answer choices, try dissecting it. Take advantage of every clue that the word might include. Prefixes and suffixes can be a huge help. Usually they allow you to determine a basic meaning. Pre- means before, post- means after, pro - is positive, de- is negative. From prefixes and suffixes, you can get an idea of the general meaning of the word and try to put it into context.

Hedge Words

Watch out for critical hedge words, such as *likely, may, can, sometimes, often, almost, mostly, usually, generally, rarely,* and *sometimes.* Question writers insert these hedge phrases to cover every possibility. Often an answer choice will be wrong simply because it leaves no room for exception. Be on guard for answer choices that have definitive words such as *exactly* and *always.*

Switchback Words

Stay alert for *switchbacks.* These are the words and phrases frequently used to alert you to shifts in thought. The most common switchback words are *but, although,* and *however.* Others include *nevertheless, on the other hand, even though, while, in spite of, despite, regardless of.* Switchback words are important to catch because they can change the direction of the question or an answer choice.

Face Value

When in doubt, use common sense. Accept the situation in the problem at face value. Don't read too much into it. These problems will not require you to make wild assumptions. If you have to go beyond creativity and warp time or space in order to have an answer choice fit the question, then you should move on and consider the other answer choices. These are normal problems rooted in reality. The applicable relationship or explanation may not be readily apparent, but it is there for you to figure out. Use your common sense to interpret anything that isn't clear.

Answer Choice Strategies

Answer Selection

The most thorough way to pick an answer choice is to identify and eliminate wrong answers until only one is left, then confirm it is the correct answer. Sometimes an answer choice may immediately seem right, but be careful. The test writers will usually put more than one reasonable answer choice on each question, so take a second to read all of them and make sure that the other choices are not equally obvious. As long as you have time left, it is better to read every answer choice than to pick the first one that looks right without checking the others.

Answer Choice Families

An answer choice family consists of two (in rare cases, three) answer choices that are very similar in construction and cannot all be true at the same time. If you see two answer choices that are direct opposites or parallels, one of them is usually the correct answer. For instance, if one answer choice says that quantity x increases and another either says that quantity x decreases (opposite) or says that quantity y increases (parallel), then those answer choices would fall into the same family. An answer choice that doesn't match the construction of the answer choice family is more likely to be incorrect. Most questions will not have answer choice families, but when they do appear, you should be prepared to recognize them.

Eliminate Answers

Eliminate answer choices as soon as you realize they are wrong, but make sure you consider all possibilities. If you are eliminating answer choices and realize that the last one you are left with is also wrong, don't panic. Start over and consider each choice again. There may be something you missed the first time that you will realize on the second pass.

Avoid Fact Traps

Don't be distracted by an answer choice that is factually true but doesn't answer the question. You are looking for the choice that answers the question. Stay focused on what the question is asking for so you don't accidentally pick an answer that is true but incorrect. Always go back to the question and make sure the answer choice you've selected actually answers the question and is not merely a true statement.

Extreme Statements

In general, you should avoid answers that put forth extreme actions as standard practice or proclaim controversial ideas as established fact. An answer choice that states the "process should be used in certain situations, if..." is much more likely to be correct than one that states the "process should be discontinued completely." The first is a calm rational statement and doesn't even make a definitive, uncompromising stance, using a hedge word *if* to provide wiggle room, whereas the second choice is a radical idea and far more extreme.

Benchmark

As you read through the answer choices and you come across one that seems to answer the question well, mentally select that answer choice. This is not your final answer, but it's the one that will help you evaluate the other answer choices. The one that you selected is your benchmark or standard for judging each of the other answer choices. Every other answer choice must be compared to your benchmark. That choice is correct until proven otherwise by another answer choice beating it. If you find a better answer, then that one becomes your new benchmark. Once you've decided that no other choice answers the question as well as your benchmark, you have your final answer.

Predict the Answer

Before you even start looking at the answer choices, it is often best to try to predict the answer. When you come up with the answer on your own, it is easier to avoid distractions and traps because you will know exactly what to look for. The right answer choice is unlikely to be word-for-word what you came up with, but it should be a close match. Even if you are confident that you have the right answer, you should still take the time to read each option before moving on.

General Strategies

Tough Questions

If you are stumped on a problem or it appears too hard or too difficult, don't waste time. Move on! Remember though, if you can quickly check for obviously incorrect answer choices, your chances of guessing correctly are greatly improved. Before you completely give up, at least try to knock out a couple of possible answers. Eliminate what you can and then guess at the remaining answer choices before moving on.

Check Your Work

Since you will probably not know every term listed and the answer to every question, it is important that you get credit for the ones that you do know. Don't miss any questions through careless mistakes. If at all possible, try to take a second to look back over your answer selection and make sure you've selected the correct answer choice and haven't made a costly careless mistake (such as marking an answer choice that you didn't mean to mark). This quick double check should more than pay for itself in caught mistakes for the time it costs.

Pace Yourself

It's easy to be overwhelmed when you're looking at a page full of questions; your mind is confused and full of random thoughts, and the clock is ticking down faster than you would like. Calm down and maintain the pace that you have set for yourself. Especially as you get down to the last few minutes of the test, don't let the small numbers on the clock make you panic. As long as you are on track by monitoring your pace, you are guaranteed to have time for each question.

struggling or have reading difficulties or disabilities. For instance, a teacher needs to be able to go back and focus on key skills and knowledge, like syllable patterns and morphemes that occur frequently. Some students need to have the same material approached from different perspectives before they fully master it. The teacher should be able to outline a number of real-world examples for an abstract concept. The use of songs and poems to illustrate syllabification is one helpful way to bring struggling students up to speed. Finally, a teacher should be able to provide differentiated practice situations for the skills that have been taught.

> **Review Video: Defining a Word**
> Visit mometrix.com/academy and enter code: 648080
>
> **Review Video: Denotation and Connotation**
> Visit mometrix.com/academy and enter code: 310092

Literal and Critical Comprehension

Literal comprehension refers to the skills a reader uses to deal with the actual words in a text. It involves skills such as identifying the topic sentence, main idea, important facts, and supporting details; using context clues to determine the meaning of a word; and sequencing events.

Critical comprehension involves prior knowledge and an understanding that written material, especially in nonfiction, is the author's version of the subject and not necessarily anybody else's. Critical comprehension involves analysis of meaning, evaluation, validation, questioning, and the reasoning skills a reader uses to recognize:

- Inferences and conclusions
- Purpose, tone, point of view, and themes
- The organizational pattern of a work
- Explicit and implicit relationships among words, phrases, and sentences
- Biased language, persuasive tactics, valid arguments, and the difference between fact and opinion

> **Review Video: Author's Main Point or Purpose**
> Visit mometrix.com/academy and enter code: 734339
>
> **Review Video: Author's Position**
> Visit mometrix.com/academy and enter code: 827954
>
> **Review Video: Inference**
> Visit mometrix.com/academy and enter code: 379203

Metacognition

Metacognition is thinking about thinking. For the student, this involves taking control of their own learning process, self-monitoring progress, evaluating the effectiveness of strategies, and making adjustments to strategies and learning behaviors as needed. Students who develop good metacognitive skills become more independent and confident about learning. They develop a sense of ownership about their education and realize that information is readily available to them.

Metacognitive skills can be grouped into three categories:

- **Awareness** – This involves identifying prior knowledge; defining learning goals; inventorying resources such as textbooks, libraries, computers, and study time; identifying task requirements and evaluation standards; and recognizing motivation and anxiety levels.
- **Planning** – This involves doing time estimates for tasks, prioritizing, scheduling study time, making checklists of tasks, gathering needed materials, and choosing strategies for problem solving or task comprehension.
- **Self-monitoring and reflection** – This involves identifying which strategies or techniques work best, questioning throughout the process, considering feedback, and maintaining focus and motivation.

Role of Metacognitive Skills in Literacy Development

In terms of literacy development, **metacognitive skills** include taking an active role in reading, recognizing reading behaviors and changing them to employ the behaviors that are most effective, relating information to prior knowledge, and being aware of text structures. For example, if there is a problem with comprehension, the student can try to form a mental image of what is described, read the text again, adjust the rate of reading, or employ other reading strategies such as identifying unknown vocabulary and predicting meaning. Being aware of **text structures** is critical to being able to follow the author's ideas and relationships among ideas. Being aware of difficulties with text structure allows the student to employ strategies such as hierarchical summaries, thematic organizers, or concept maps to remedy the problem.

Critical Thinking Tools

It is important to teach students to use critical thinking skills when reading. Three of the **critical thinking tools** that engage the reader are:

- **Summarization** – The student reviews the main point(s) of the reading selection and identifies important details. For nonfiction, a good summary will briefly describe the main arguments and the examples that support those arguments. For fiction, a good summary will identify the main characters and events of the story.
- **Question generation** – A good reader will constantly ask questions while reading about comprehension, vocabulary, connections to personal knowledge or experience, predictions, etc.
- **Textual marking** – This skill engages the reader by having him or her interact with the text. The student should mark the text with questions or comments that are generated by the text using underlining, highlighting, or shorthand marks such as "?," "!," and "*" that indicate lack of understanding, importance, or key points, for example.

Context Clues

Context clues are words or phrases that help the reader figure out the meaning of an unknown word. They are built into a sentence or paragraph by the writer to help the reader develop a clear understanding of the writer's message. Context clues can be used to make **intelligent guesses**

about the meaning of a word instead of relying on a dictionary. Context clues are the reason most vocabulary is learned through reading. There are four types of commonly used context clues:

- **Synonyms** – A word with the same meaning as the unknown word is placed close by for comparison.
- **Antonyms** – A word with the opposite meaning as the unknown word is placed close by for contrast.
- **Explanations** – An obvious explanation is given close to the unknown word.
- **Examples** – Examples of what the word means are given to help the reader define the term.

> **Review Video: Synonyms and Antonyms**
> Visit mometrix.com/academy and enter code: 105612
>
> **Review Video: Multiple Meaning Words**
> Visit mometrix.com/academy and enter code: 371666

Topic Sentence

The **topic sentence** of a paragraph states the paragraph's subject. It presents the **main idea**. The rest of the paragraph should be related to the topic sentence, which should be explained and supported with facts, details, proofs, and examples. The topic sentence is more general than the **body sentences**, and should cover all the ideas in the body of the paragraph. It may contain words such as "many," "most," or "several." The topic sentence is usually the first sentence in a paragraph, but it can appear after an introductory or background sentence, can be the last sentence in a paragraph, or may simply be implied, meaning a topic sentence is not present. **Supporting sentences** can often be identified by their use of transition terms such as "for example" or "that is." Supporting sentences may also be presented in numbered sequence. The topic sentence provides **unity** to a paragraph because it ties together the supporting details into a coherent whole.

> **Review Video: Topics and Main Ideas**
> Visit mometrix.com/academy and enter code: 407801
>
> **Review Video: Supporting Details**
> Visit mometrix.com/academy and enter code: 396297

Theme

Theme is the central idea of a work. It is the thread that ties all the elements of a story together and gives them purpose. The theme is not the subject of a work, but what a work says about a subject. A theme must be **universal**, which means it must apply to everyone, not just the characters in a story. Therefore, a theme is a comment about the nature of humanity, society, the relationship of humankind to the world, or moral responsibility. There may be more than one theme in a work, and the determination of the theme is affected by the viewpoint of the reader. Therefore, there is not always necessarily a definite, irrefutable theme. The theme can be implied or stated directly.

> **Review Video: Theme**
> Visit mometrix.com/academy and enter code: 732074

Types of Definition Paragraphs or Essays

A **definition paragraph** or essay describes what a word or term means. There are three ways the explanation can be presented:

- **Definition by synonym** – The term is defined by comparing it to a more familiar term that the reader can more easily understand (A phantom is a ghost or spirit that appears and disappears mysteriously and creates dread).
- **Definition by class** – Most commonly used in exams, papers, and reports, the class definition first puts the term in a larger category or class (The Hereford is a breed of cattle), and then describes the distinguishing characteristics or details of the term that differentiate it from other members of the class (The Hereford is a breed of cattle distinguished by a white face, reddish-brown hide, and short horns).
- **Definition by negation** – The term is defined by stating what it is not and then saying what it is (Courage is not the absence of fear, but the willingness to act in spite of fear).

Types of Paragraphs and Essays

Illustrative — An illustrative paragraph or essay explains a general statement through the use of specific examples. The writer starts with a topic sentence that is followed by one or more examples that clearly relate to and support the topic.

Narrative — A narrative tells a story. Like a news report, it tells the who, what, when, where, why, and how of an event. A narrative is usually presented in chronological order.

Descriptive — This type of writing appeals to the five senses to describe a person, place, or thing so that the readers can see the subject in their imaginations. Space order is most often used in descriptive writing to indicate place or position.

Process — There are two kinds of process papers: the "how-to" that gives step-by-step directions on how to do something and the explanation paper that tells how an event occurred or how something works.

> **Review Video: Reading Essays**
> Visit mometrix.com/academy and enter code: 169166

Cause and Effect

Causes are reasons for actions or events. **Effects** are the results of a cause or causes. There may be multiple causes for one effect (evolutionary extinction, climate changes, and a massive comet caused the demise of the dinosaurs, for example) or multiple effects from one cause (the break-up of the Soviet Union has had multiple effects on the world stage, for instance). Sometimes, one thing leads to another and the effect of one action becomes the cause for another (breaking an arm leads to not driving, which leads to reading more while staying home, for example). The ability to identify causes and effects is part of critical thinking, and enables the reader to follow the course of events, make connections among events, and identify the instigators and receivers of actions. This ability improves comprehension.

> **Review Video: Cause and Effect**
> Visit mometrix.com/academy and enter code: 428037
>
> **Review Video: Rhetorical Strategy of Cause-and-Effect Analysis**
> Visit mometrix.com/academy and enter code: 725944

Distinguishing Between Facts and Opinions

Facts are statements that can be verified through research. Facts answer the questions of who, what, when, and where, and evidence can be provided to prove factual statements. For example, it is a fact that water turns into ice when the temperature drops below 32 degrees Fahrenheit. This fact has been proven repeatedly. Water never becomes ice at a higher temperature. **Opinions** are personal views, but facts may be used to support opinions. For example, it may be one person's opinion that Jack is a great athlete, but the fact that he has made many achievements related to sports supports that opinion. It is important for a reader to be able to distinguish between fact and opinion to determine the validity of an argument. Readers need to understand that some unethical writers will try to pass off an opinion as a fact. Readers with good critical thinking skills will not be deceived by this tactic.

> **Review Video: Fact or Opinion**
> Visit mometrix.com/academy and enter code: 870899
>
> **Review Video: Text Evidence**
> Visit mometrix.com/academy and enter code: 486236

Inductive and Deductive Reasoning

Inductive reasoning is using particulars to draw a general conclusion. The inductive reasoning process starts with **data**. For example, if every apple taken out of the top of a barrel is rotten, it can be inferred without investigating further that all the apples are probably rotten. Unless all data is examined, conclusions are based on probabilities. Inductive reasoning is also used to make inferences about the universe. The entire universe cannot be examined, but inferences can be made based on observations about what can be seen. These inferences may be proven false when more data is available, but they are valid at the time they are made if observable data is used. **Deductive reasoning** is the opposite of inductive reasoning. It involves using general facts or premises to come to a specific conclusion. For example, if Susan is a sophomore in high school, and all sophomores take geometry, it can be inferred that Susan takes geometry. The word "all" does not allow for exceptions. If all sophomores take geometry, assuming Susan does too is a logical conclusion. It is important for a reader to recognize inductive and deductive reasoning so he or she can follow the line of an argument and determine if the inference or conclusion is **valid**.

Style, Tone, and Point of View

Style is the manner in which a writer uses language in prose or poetry. Style is affected by:

- Diction or word choices
- Sentence structure and syntax
- Types and extent of use of figurative language

- Patterns of rhythm or sound
- Conventional or creative use of punctuation

Tone is the attitude of the writer or narrator towards the theme of, subject of, or characters in a work. Sometimes the attitude is stated, but it is most often implied through word choices. Examples of tone are serious, humorous, satiric, stoic, cynical, flippant, and surprised.

Point of view is the angle from which a story is told. It is the perspective of the narrator, established by the author. Common points of view are:

- *Third person* – Third person points of view include omniscient (knows everything) and limited (confined to what is known by a single character or a limited number of characters). When the third person is used, characters are referred to as he, she, or they.
- *First person* – When this point of view is used, the narrator refers to himself or herself as "I."

> **Review Video: Style, Tone, and Mood**
> Visit mometrix.com/academy and enter code: 416961
>
> **Review Video: Point of View**
> Visit mometrix.com/academy and enter code: 383336

Types of Figurative Language

A **simile** is a comparison between two unlike things using the words "like" or "as." Examples are Robert Burn's sentence "O my love's like a red, red, rose" or the common expression "as pretty as a picture."

A **metaphor** is a direct comparison between two unlike things without the use of "like" or "as." One thing is identified as the other instead of simply compared to it. An example is D. H. Lawrence's sentence "My soul is a dark forest."

Personification is the giving of human characteristics to a non-human thing or idea. An example is "The hurricane howled its frightful rage."

Synecdoche is the use of a part of something to signify the whole. For example, "boots on the ground" could be used to describe soldiers in a field.

Metonymy is the use of one term that is closely associated with another to mean the other. An example is referring to the "crown" to refer to the monarchy.

Alliteration, Assonance, and Onomatopoeia

Alliteration is the repetition of the first sounds or stressed syllables (usually consonants) in words in close proximity. An example is: "Chirp, chirp," said the chickadee.

Assonance is the repetition of identical or similar vowel sounds, particularly in stressed syllables, in words in close proximity. Assonance is considered to be a form of near rhyme. An example is: the quiet bride cried.

Onomatopoeia refers to words that imitate sounds. It is sometimes called echoism. Examples are hiss, buzz, burp, rattle, and pop. It may also refer to words that correspond symbolically to what they describe, with high tones suggesting light and low tones suggesting darkness. An example is the *gloom* of night versus the *gleam* of the stars.

22

well as reading levels for this group vary. Reading levels will usually range from 6.0 to 8.9. Examples of popular literature for this age group and reading level include:

- Series – Sweet Valley High, Bluford High, Nancy Drew, Hardy Boys, and Little House on the Prairie
- Juvenile fiction authors – Judy Blume and S. E. Hinton
- Fantasy and horror authors – Ursula LeGuin and Stephen King
- Science fiction authors – Isaac Asimov, Ray Bradbury, and H. G. Wells
- Classic books: Lilies of the Field, Charlie and the Chocolate Factory, Pippi Longstocking, National Velvet, Call of the Wild, Anne of Green Gables, The Hobbit, The Member of the Wedding, and Tom Sawyer

Writing Process and Applications

Grammatical Terms

The definitions for grammatical terms are as follows:

Adjective – This is a word that modifies or describes a noun or pronoun. Examples are a *green* apple or *every* computer.

Adverb – This is a word that modifies a verb (*instantly* reviewed), an adjective (*relatively* odd), or another adverb (*rather* suspiciously).

Conjunctions: There are three types of conjunctions:

- **Coordinating conjunctions** are used to link words, phrases, and clauses. Examples are and, or, nor, for, but, yet, and so.
- **Correlative conjunctions** are paired terms used to link clauses. Examples are either/or, neither/nor, and if/then.
- **Subordinating conjunctions** relate subordinate or dependent clauses to independent ones. Examples are although, because, if, since, before, after, when, even though, in order that, and while.

Gerund – This is a verb form used as a noun. Most end in "ing." An example is: *Walking* is good exercise.

Infinitive – This is a verbal form comprised of the word "to" followed by the root form of a verb. An infinitive may be used as a noun, adjective, adverb, or absolute. Examples include:

- *To hold* a baby is a joy. (noun)
- Jenna had many files *to reorganize*. (adjective)
- Andrew tried *to remember* the dates. (adverb)
- *To be honest*, your hair looks awful. (absolute)

Noun – This is a word that names a person, place, thing, idea, or quality. A noun can be used as a subject, object, complement, appositive, or modifier.

Object – This is a word or phrase that receives the action of a verb.

- A direct object states *to* whom/what an action was committed. It answers the question "to what?" An example is: Joan served *the meal*.
- An indirect object states *for* whom/what an action was committed. An example is: Joan served *us* the meal.

Preposition – This is a word that links a noun or pronoun to other parts of a sentence. Examples include above, by, for, in, out, through, and to.

Prepositional phrase – This is a combination of a preposition and a noun or pronoun. Examples include across the bridge, against the grain, below the horizon, and toward the sunset.

Pronoun – This is a word that represents a specific noun in a generic way. A pronoun functions like a noun in a sentence. Examples include I, she, he, it, myself, they, these, what, all, and anybody.

28

Sentence – This is a group of words that expresses a thought or conveys information as an independent unit of speech. A **complete sentence** must contain a noun and a verb (I ran). However, all the other parts of speech can also be represented in a sentence.

Verb – This is a word or phrase in a sentence that expresses action (Mary played) or a state of being (Mary is).

> **Review Video: Parts of Speech**
> Visit mometrix.com/academy and enter code: 899611

Capitalization and Punctuation

Capitalization refers to the use of capital letters. Capital letters should be placed at the beginning of:

- **Proper names** (Ralph Waldo Emerson, Australia)
- **Places** (Mount Rushmore, Chicago)
- Historical periods and holidays (Renaissance, Christmas)
- **Religious terms** (Bible, Koran)
- **Titles** (Empress Victoria, General Smith)
- All main words in **literary, art, or music titles** (Grapes of Wrath, Sonata in C Major)

Punctuation consists of:

Periods – A period is placed at the end of a sentence.

Commas – A comma is used to separate:

- Two adjectives modifying the same word (long, hot summer)
- Three or more words or phrases in a list (Winken, Blinken, and Nod; life, liberty, and the pursuit of happiness)
- Phrases that are not needed to complete a sentence (The teacher, not the students, will distribute the supplies.)

Colons and Semicolons

Colons – A colon is used to:

- Set up a **list** (We will need these items: a pencil, paper, and an eraser.)
- Direct readers to **examples or explanations** (We have one chore left: clean out the garage.)
- Introduce **quotations or dialogue** (The Labor Department reported on unemployment: "There was a 3.67% increase in unemployment in 2010."; Scarlett exclaimed: "What shall I do?")

> **Review Video: Colons**
> Visit mometrix.com/academy and enter code: 868673

29

Semicolons – A semicolon is used to:

- Join **related independent clauses** (There were five major hurricanes this year; two of them hit Florida.)
- Join **independent clauses connected by conjunctive adverbs** (Popular books are often made into movies; however, it is a rare screenplay that is as good as the book.)
- Separate items in a **series** if commas would be confusing (The characters include: Robin Hood, who robs from the rich to give to the poor; Maid Marian, his true love; and Little John, Robin Hood's comrade-in-arms.)

> **Review Video: Semicolon Usage**
> Visit mometrix.com/academy and enter code: 370605

Subject-Verb Agreement

A verb must **agree** in number with its subject. Therefore, a verb changes form depending on whether the subject is singular or plural. Examples include "I do," "he does," "the ball is," and "the balls are." If two subjects are joined by "and," the **plural** form of a verb is usually used. For example: *Jack and Jill want* to get some water (Jack wants, Jill wants, but together they want). If the compound subjects are preceded by each or every, they take the **singular** form of a verb. For example: *Each man and each woman brings* a special talent to the world (each brings, not bring). If one noun in a compound subject is plural and the other is singular, the verb takes the form of the subject **nearest** to it. For example: Neither the *students* nor their *teacher was* ready for the fire drill. **Collective nouns** that name a group are considered singular if they refer to the group acting as a unit. For example: The *choir is going* on a concert tour.

> **Review Video: Subject Verb Agreement**
> Visit mometrix.com/academy and enter code: 479190

Syntax

Syntax refers to the rules related to how to properly **structure** sentences and phrases. Syntax is not the same as grammar. For example, "I does" is syntactically correct because the subject and verb are in proper order, but it is grammatically incorrect because the subject and verb don't agree.

There are three types of sentence structures:

- **Simple** – This type is composed of a single independent clause with one subject and one predicate (verb or verb form).
- **Compound** – This type is composed of two independent clauses joined by a conjunction (Amy flew, but Brenda took the train), a correlative conjunction (Either Tom goes with me or I stay here), or a semicolon (My grandfather stays in shape; he plays tennis nearly every day).
- **Complex** – This type is composed of one independent clause and one or more dependent clauses joined by a subordinating conjunction (Before we set the table, we should replace the tablecloth).

Types of Paragraphs or Essays

A **comparison and contrast essay** examines the similarities and differences between two things. In a paragraph, the writer presents all the points about subject A and then all the points about

30

- Children will make some attempt to use **vowels** in writing.
- Children will write with more ease, although spelling will still be phonetic and only some punctuation will be used.

Journal Writing

Writing in a **journal** gives students practice in writing, which makes them more comfortable with the writing process. Journal writing also gives students the opportunity to sort out their thoughts, solve problems, examine relationships and values, and see their personal and academic growth when they revisit old entries. The advantages for the teacher are that the students become more experienced with and accustomed to writing. Through reading student journals, the teacher can also gain **insight** into the students' problems and attitudes, which can help the teacher tailor his or her lesson plans. A journal can be kept in a **notebook** or in a **computer file**. It shouldn't be just a record of daily events, but an expression of thoughts and feelings about everything and anything. Grammar and punctuation don't matter since journaling is a form of private communication. Teachers who review journals need to keep in mind that they should not grade journals and that comments should be encouraging and polite.

Revising a Paper

Revising a paper involves rethinking the choices that were made while constructing the paper and then rewriting it, making any necessary changes or additions to word choices or arrangement of points. Questions to keep in mind include:

- Is the thesis clear?
- Do the body paragraphs logically flow and provide details to support the thesis?
- Is anything unnecessarily repeated?
- Is there anything not related to the topic?
- Is the language understandable?
- Does anything need to be defined?
- Is the material interesting?

Another consideration when revising is **peer feedback**. It is helpful during the revision process to have someone who is knowledgeable enough to be helpful and will be willing to give an honest critique read the paper.

> **Review Video: General Revision and Proofreading**
> Visit mometrix.com/academy and enter code: 385882

Paragraph Coherence

Paragraph coherence can be achieved by linking sentences by using the following strategies:

- **Repetition of key words** – It helps the reader follow the progression of thought from one sentence to another if key words (which should be defined) are repeated to assure the reader that the writer is still on topic and the discussion still relates to the key word.
- **Substitution of pronouns** – This doesn't just refer to using single word pronouns such as I, they, us, etc., but also alternate descriptions of the subject. For example, if someone was writing about Benjamin Franklin, it gets boring to keep saying Franklin or he. Other terms that describe him, such as that notable American statesman, this printer, the inventor, and so forth can also be used.

35

- **Substitution of synonyms** – This is similar to substitution of pronouns, but refers to using similar terms for any repeated noun or adjective, not just the subject. For example, instead of constantly using the word great, adjectives such as terrific, really cool, awesome, and so on can also be used.

Verbs

In order to understand the role of a verb and be able to identify the verb that is necessary to make a sentence, it helps to know the different types of verbs. These are:

- **Action verbs** – These are verbs that express an action being performed by the subject. An example is: The outfielder caught the ball (outfielder = subject and caught = action).
- **Linking verbs** – These are verbs that link the subject to words that describe or identify the subject. An example is: Mary is an excellent teacher (Mary = subject and "is" links Mary to her description as an excellent teacher). Common linking verbs are all forms of the verb "to be," appear, feel, look, become, and seem.
- **Helping verbs** – When a single verb cannot do the job by itself because of tense issues, a second, helping verb is added. Examples include: should have gone ("gone" is the main verb, while "should" and "have" are helping verbs), and was playing ("playing" is the main verb, while "was" is the helping verb).

Coordinating Conjunctions and Subordinating Conjunctions

There are different ways to connect two clauses and show their relationship:

- A **coordinating conjunction** is one that can join two independent clauses by placing a comma and a coordinating conjunction between them. The most common coordinating conjunctions are and, but, or, nor, yet, for, and so. Examples include: "It was warm, so I left my jacket at home" and "It was warm, and I left my jacket at home."
- A **subordinating conjunction** is one that joins a subordinate clause and an independent clause and establishes the relationship between them. An example is: "We can play a game after Steve finishes his homework." The dependent clause is "after Steve finishes his homework" because the reader immediately asks, "After Steve finishes, then what?" The independent clause is "We can play a game." The concern is not the ability to play a game, but "when?" The answer to this question is dependent on when Steve finishes his homework.

> **Review Video: Conjunctions**
> Visit mometrix.com/academy and enter code: 904603

Run-On Sentences and Comma Splices

A **run-on sentence** is one that tries to connect two independent clauses without the needed conjunction or punctuation and makes it hard for the reader to figure out where one sentence ends and the other starts. An example is: "Meagan is three years old she goes to pre-school." Two possible ways to fix the run-on would be: "Meagan is three years old, and she goes to pre-school" or "Meagan is three years old; however, she goes to pre-school." A **comma splice** occurs when a comma is used to join two independent clauses without a proper conjunction. The comma should be replaced by a period or one of the methods for coordination or subordination should be used. An example of a comma splice is: "Meagan is three years old, she goes to pre-school."

Fragments

A **fragment** is an incomplete sentence, which is one that does not have a subject to go with the verb, or vice versa. The following are types of fragments:

- **Dependent clause fragments** – These usually start with a subordinating conjunction. An example is: "Before you can graduate." "You can graduate" is a sentence, but the subordinating conjunction "before" makes the clause dependent, which means it needs an independent clause to go with it. An example is: "Before you can graduate, you have to meet all the course requirements."
- **Relative clause fragments** – These often start with who, whose, which, or that. An example is: "Who is always available to the students." This is a fragment because the "who" is not identified. A complete sentence would be: "Mr. Jones is a principal who is always available to the students."
- **The "-ing" fragment** lacks a subject. The "-ing" form of a verb has to have a helping verb. An example is: "Walking only three blocks to his job." A corrected sentence would be: "Walking only three blocks to his job, Taylor has no need for a car."
- **Prepositional phrase fragments** are ones that begin with a preposition and are only a phrase, not a complete thought. An example is: "By the time we arrived." "We arrived" by itself would be a complete sentence, but the "by" makes the clause dependent and the reader asks, "By the time you arrived, what happened?" A corrected sentence would be: "By the time we arrived, all the food was gone."
- **Infinitive phrase fragments** have the same problem as prepositional phrase ones. An example is: "To plant the seed." A corrected sentence would be: "To plant the seed, Isaac used a trowel."

> **Review Video: Fragments and Run-on Sentences**
> Visit mometrix.com/academy and enter code: 541989

Primary and Secondary Research Information

Primary research material is material that comes from the "horse's mouth." It is a document or object that was created by the person under study or during the time period under study. Examples of primary sources are original documents such as manuscripts, diaries, interviews, autobiographies, government records, letters, news videos, and artifacts (such as Native American pottery or wall writings in Egyptian tombs). **Secondary research material** is anything that is not primary. Secondary sources are those things that are written or otherwise recorded about the main subject. Examples include a critical analysis of a literary work (a poem by William Blake is primary, but the analysis of the poem by T. S. Eliot is secondary), a magazine article about a person (a direct quote would be primary, but the report is secondary), histories, commentaries, and encyclopedias.

Primary sources are the raw material of research. This can include results of experiments, notes, and surveys or interviews done by the researcher. Other primary sources are books, letters, diaries, eyewitness accounts, and performances attended by the researcher. **Secondary sources** consist of oral and written accounts prepared by others. This includes reports, summaries, critical reviews, and other sources not developed by the researcher. Most research writing uses both primary and secondary sources: primary sources from first-hand accounts and secondary sources for background and supporting documentation. The research process calls for active reading and writing throughout. As research yields information, it often calls for more reading and research, and the cycle continues.

37

Drafting Research Essays

<u>Introduction</u>

The **introduction** to a research essay is particularly important, as it sets the *context* for the essay. It needs to draw the reader into the subject and provide necessary background to understand the subject. It is sometimes helpful to open with the research question and explain how the question will be answered. The major points of the essay may be forecast or previewed to prepare readers for the coming arguments. In a research essay, it is a good idea to establish the writer's credibility by reviewing credentials and experience with the subject. Another useful opening involves quoting several sources that support the points of the essay, again to establish credibility. The tone should be appropriate to the audience and subject, maintaining a sense of careful authority while building the arguments. *Jargon* should be kept to a minimum, and language should be carefully chosen to reflect the appropriate tone.

<u>Conclusion</u>

The **conclusion** to a research essay helps readers summarize what they have learned. Conclusions are not meant to convince, as this has been done in the body of the essay. It can be useful to leave the reader with a memorable phrase or example that supports the argument. Conclusions should be both memorable and logical restatements of the arguments in the body of the essay. A *specific-to-general pattern* can be helpful, opening with the thesis statement and expanding to more general observations. A good idea is to restate the main points in the body of the essay, leading to the conclusion. An ending that evokes a vivid image or asks a provocative question makes the essay memorable. The same effect can be achieved by a call for action, or a warning. Conclusions may be tailored to the audience's background, in terms of language, tone, and style.

<u>Reviewing the Draft</u>

Checklist for Reviewing a Draft of a Research Essay

1. **Introduction**: Is the reader's attention gained and held by the introduction?
2. **Thesis**: Does the essay fulfill the promise of the thesis? Is it strong enough?
3. **Main points**: Are the main points listed and ranked in order of importance?
4. **Organization**: What is the organizing principle of the essay? Does it work?
5. **Supporting information**: Is the thesis adequately supported? Is the thesis convincing?
6. **Source material**: Are there adequate sources and are they smoothly integrated into the essay?
7. **Conclusion**: Does the conclusion have sufficient power? Does it summarize the essay well?
8. **Paragraphs, sentences, words**: Are these elements effective in promoting the thesis?
9. **Overall review**: Evaluate the essay's strengths and weaknesses. What revisions are needed?

Modern Language Association Style

The **Modern Language Association style** is widely used in literature and languages as well as other fields. The MLA style calls for noting brief references to sources in parentheses in the text of an essay and adding an alphabetical list of sources, called "Works Cited," at the end. Specific recommendations of the MLA include the following:

1. "**Works Cited**": Include in this section only works actually cited. List on a separate page the author's name, title, and publication information, which must include the location of the publisher, the publisher's name, and the date of publication.

Civics and Economics

The Civil Rights Act of 1871

The Civil Rights Act of 1871 was a statue passed following the Civil War. It was comprised of the **1870 Force Act** and the **1871 Ku Klux Klan Act**. It was passed primarily with the intention of protecting southern blacks from the Ku Klux Klan. Since it was passed in 1871, the statute has only undergone small changes. It has however, been interpreted widely by the courts. In 1882 some parts of the Civil Rights Act of 1871 were found unconstitutional, but the Force Act and the Klan Act continued to be applied in civil rights cases in subsequent years.

Plessy v. Ferguson

Plessy v. Ferguson was an 1896 Supreme Court case. The case resulted in the decision that **de jure racial segregation** in **public facilities** was legal in the United States, and permitted states to restrict blacks from using public facilities. The case originated when, in 1890, a black man named Homer Plessy decided to challenge a Louisiana law that segregated blacks and whites on trains by sitting in the white section of a train. Plessy was convicted of breaking the law in a Louisiana court, and the case was appealed to the U.S. Supreme Court, where the Supreme Court upheld the Louisiana decision. The case established the legality of the doctrine of separate but equal, thereby allowing racial segregation. The decision was later overturned by **Brown versus the Board of Education of Topeka**.

The Fair Employment Act

The Fair Employment Act was signed by President Franklin Roosevelt in 1941. The purpose of the act was to **ban racial discrimination** in industries related to **national defense** and represented the very first federal law to ban discrimination in employment. The **Fair Employment Act** mandated that all federal government agencies and departments concerned with national defense, as well as private defense contractors, guaranteed that professional training would be conducted without discrimination based on race, creed, color, or national origin. The Fair Employment Act was followed by **Title VII of the 1964 Civil Rights Act**, which banned discrimination by private employers, and by **Executive Order 11246** in 1965, which concerned federal contractors and subcontractors.

Brown v. Board of Education

Brown versus the Board of Education of Topeka was a Supreme Court case that was decided in 1954. The case made it illegal for **racial segregation** to exist within **public education facilities**. This decision was based on the finding that separate but equal public educational facilities would not provide black and white students with the same standard of facilities. The case originated in 1951, when a lawsuit was filed by Topeka parents, who were recruited by the NAACP, against the Board of Education of the City of Topeka, Kansas in a U.S. District Court. The parents, one of whom was named Oliver Brown, wanted the Topeka Board of Education to eliminate racial segregation. The District Court agreed that segregation had negative effects, but did not force the schools to desegregate because it found that black and white school facilities in the District were generally equal in standards. The case was appealed to the Supreme Court, where the finding was that separate educational facilities are unequal.

Bolling v. Sharpe

Bolling v. Sharpe was a 1954 Supreme Court case. Like Brown v. Board of Education, this case addressed issues concerning **segregation in public schools**. The case originated in 1949, when parents from Anacostia, an area in Washington, DC, petitioned the Board of Education of the District of Columbia to allow all races to attend a new school. The request was denied. A lawsuit was brought before the District Court for the District of Columbia on behalf of a student named Bolling and other students to admit them to the all-white school. The case was dismissed by the District Court and taken to the Supreme Court. The Supreme Court ruled that the school had to be desegregated based on the Fifth Amendment.

Civil Rights Act of 1964

The Civil Rights Act of 1964 was passed to protect the right of both **black men** and of **women**. It served as part of the foundation for the women's right movement. The act was a catalyst for change in the United States, as it made it illegal to engage in acts of **discrimination** in public facilities, in government, and in employment. The Civil Rights Act prohibited unequal voter registration, prohibited discrimination in all public facilities involved in interstate commerce, supported desegregating public schools, insured equal protection for blacks in federally funded programs, and banned employment discrimination.

The Pregnancy Discrimination Act

The Pregnancy Discrimination Act was passed in 1978 as an amendment to the sex discrimination clause of the Civil Rights Act of 1964. The **Pregnancy Discrimination Act** stipulated that people cannot be discriminated against due to pregnancy, childbirth, or medical issues related to pregnancy or childbirth. If a person becomes pregnant, gives birth, or has related medical conditions they must receive treatment that is equivalent to that received by other employees and also receive equal benefits as other employees. The **Family and Medical Leave Act** was passed in 1993 to advance protections under the Pregnancy Discrimination Act.

Civil Rights Act of 1968

The Civil Rights Act of 1968 was passed following the passing of the Civil Rights Act of 1964. The act made it illegal to **discriminate** against individuals during the sale, rental, or financing of **housing**. Therefore, the act is also referred to as the **Fair Housing Act of 1968**. The act made it illegal to refuse to sell or rent housing based on race, color, religion, or national origin. It also made it illegal to advertise housing for sale or rent and to specify a preference to rent or sell the property to an individual of a particular race, color, religion, or national origin. In addition, the act ensured protection for civil rights workers.

Age Discrimination in Employment Act

The Age Discrimination in Employment Act of 1967 makes it illegal for employers to discriminate against people who are **forty years old** or greater in age. The act establishes standards for employer provided pensions and benefits and mandates that information regarding the needs of older workers be made publicly available. In addition to generally banning age discrimination, the **ADEA** specifies particular actions that are illegal. Employers may not specify that individuals of a certain age are preferred or are conversely restricted from applying to job ads. Age limits are only permitted to be mentioned in job ads if age has been shown to be a bona fide occupational qualification. The act stipulates that it is illegal to discriminate against age through apprenticeship programs, and that it is illegal to restrict benefits to older employees. However, employers are

permitted to lower the benefits provided to older employees based on age if the expense of providing fewer or lesser benefits is equivalent to the expense of providing benefits to younger employees.

Loving v. Virginia

Loving versus Virginia was a 1967 Supreme Court case. The decision that resulted from the case ruled that a particular law in Virginia known as the **Racial Integrity Act of 1924** was unconstitutional. The Virginia law had prohibited interracial marriage, and therefore with the Supreme Court ruling put an end to **race-based restrictions on marriage**. The case originated when Mildred Jeter and Richard Loving, an interracial Virginia couple that was married in Washington, D.C. due to a Virginia state law prohibiting interracial marriage returned to Virginia and received charges of violating the interracial marriage ban. After pleading guilty, the couple was forced to move to D.C. to avoid a jail sentence, where they brought their case to the Supreme Court on the premise that their Fourteenth Amendment rights had been violated. The Supreme Court found that the Virginia law was unconstitutional and overturned the conviction that the couple had been charged with.

Jones v. Mayer

Jones versus Mayer was a 1968 Supreme Court case. In this case, the United States Supreme Court ruled that Congress has the authority to **regulate the sale of private property** for the purpose of preventing racial discrimination. This United States Supreme Court ruling was based on a legal statue that stipulates that it is illegal in the United States to commit acts of racial discrimination, both privately and publicly, when selling or renting property. The United States Supreme Court ruled that the Congressional power to uphold the statute extends from the power of Congress to uphold the Thirteenth Amendment.

Roe v. Wade

Roe v. Wade was a controversial 1973 U.S. Supreme Court case. The case originated in 1970 in Texas, which had an **anti-abortion law**. The plaintiff was an unmarried pregnant woman who was assigned the name "Jane Roe" to protect her identity. Texas anti-abortion law characterized the acts of having or attempting to perform an abortion as crimes, with the exception of cases in which an abortion could save the life of a mother. The lawsuit argued that the Texas law was unconstitutionally vague and was not consistent with the rights guaranteed by the First, Fourth, Fifth, Ninth, and Fourteenth Amendments. While the Texas court ruled in favor of Roe, it did not rule that Texas had to discontinue the enforcement of its anti-abortion law. Roe appealed to the Supreme Court in 1971, and the court's decision in 1973 struck down Texas's abortion laws. The case overturned most state laws prohibiting abortion.

Regents of the University of California v. Bakke

Regents of the University of California versus Bakke was a 1978 Supreme Court case that banned **quota systems** in the college admissions process but ruled that programs providing **advantages to minorities** are constitutionally sound. The case originated when Allan Bakke, a white male who was a strong student, applied to the University of California at Davis Medical School and was rejected. The school had a program that reserved admissions spots for minority applicants; the program had grown along with the overall size of the school since its opening in 1968. Bakke complained to the school but was still not admitted and he finally brought his case before the Superior Court of California. The California court ruled in favor of Bakke, who claimed that he had been discriminated against because of his race, and the school appealed to the U.S. Supreme Court.

The Supreme Court ruled that race could be used as one factor by discriminatory boards such as college admissions boards, however quotas were ruled to be **discriminatory**.

Americans with Disabilities Act (ADA)

The ADA was passed by Congress in 1990. This act outlines the rights of individuals with disabilities in society in all ways besides education. It states that they should receive **nondiscriminatory treatment** in jobs, **access** to businesses and other stores, and other services. Due to this law, all businesses must be wheelchair accessible, having a ramp that fits the standards of the law, and making sure that all doors are wide enough and that bathrooms can be maneuvered by someone in a wheelchair. If these rules are not followed, businesses can be subject to large fines until these modifications have been complied with. The ADA also ensures fair treatment when applying for jobs to make sure that there is no unfair discrimination for any person with a disability who is applying to the job.

The Civil Rights Act of 1991

The Civil Rights Act of 1991 is a statute. It was passed as a result of a number of Supreme Court decisions that restricted the rights of individuals who had sued their employers on the basis of discrimination. The passing of the **Civil Rights Act of 1991** was the first time since the Civil Rights Act of 1964 was passed that modifications were made to the rights granted under federal laws to individuals in cases involving **employment discrimination**. Specifically, the Civil Rights Act of 1991 granted the right to a trial by jury to individuals involved in cases of employment discrimination and it also addressed for the first time the potential for emotional distress damages and limited the amount awarded by a jury in such cases.

Planned Parenthood v. Casey

Planned Parenthood of Southeastern Pennsylvania v. Casey was a 1992 Supreme Court case that challenged the constitutionality of Pennsylvania abortion laws. The case was brought before the U.S. District Court for the Eastern District of Pennsylvania by abortion clinics and physicians to challenge four clauses of the **Pennsylvania Abortion Control Act of 1982** as unconstitutional under Roe v. Wade. The District Court ruled that all of the clauses of the Pennsylvania act were unconstitutional. The case was then appealed to the Third Circuit Court of Appeals, which ruled to uphold all of the clauses except for one requiring notification of a husband prior to abortion. The case was then appealed to the Supreme Court, which ruled to uphold constitutional right to have an abortion, thereby upholding Roe v. Wade.

Adarand Constructors, Inc. v. Peña

Adarand Constructors, Inc. versus Peña was a 1995 United States Supreme Court case in which the court ruled that any **racial classifications** that are instituted by representatives of federal, state, or local governments have to be reviewed and analyzed by a court. The court that reviews such racial classifications must abide by a policy of **strict scrutiny**. Strict scrutiny represents the highest standard of Supreme Court review. Racial classifications are deemed constitutional solely under circumstances in which they are being used as specific measures to advance critical and important governmental interests. The ruling of the Supreme Court in this case requiring strict scrutiny as a standard of review for racial classifications overturned the case of **Metro Broadcasting, Inc. v. FCC**, in which the Supreme Court established a two-level method of reviewing and analyzing racial classifications.

The Employment Non-Discrimination Act

The Employment Non-Discrimination Act is a proposed United States federal law that has not yet been passed. The **Employment Non-Discrimination Act** would ban employers from discriminating against their employees based on their **sexual orientation**. A number of states have already passed laws that ban discrimination based on sexual orientation, including California, Connecticut, the District of Columbia, Hawaii, Maryland, Massachusetts, Minnesota, Nevada, New Hampshire, New Jersey, New Mexico, New York, Rhode Island, Vermont, and Wisconsin. As it is currently proposed, the federal law would not protect transgender or intersexual individuals from discrimination.

Public Policy

Public policy is the study of how the various levels of government formulate and implement policies. **Public policy** also refers to the set of policies that a government adopts and implements, including laws, plans, actions, and behaviors, for the purpose of governing society. Public policy is developed and adapted through the process of **policy analysis**. Public policy analysis is the systematic evaluation of alternative means of reaching social goals. Public policy is divided into various policy areas, including domestic policy, foreign policy, healthcare policy, education policy, criminal policy, national defense policy, and energy policy.

Grutter v. Bollinger

Grutter versus Bollinger was a 2003 Supreme Court case that upheld an **affirmative action policy** of the University of Michigan Law School admissions process. The case originated in 1996 when Barbara Grutter, a white in-state resident with a strong academic record applied to the law school and was denied admission. In 1997 she filed a lawsuit claiming that her rejection was based on racial discrimination and violated her Fourteenth Amendment rights, as well as Title VI of the Civil Rights Act of 1964. The case was heard in 2001 in a U.S. District Court, which ruled that the university's admissions policies were unconstitutional. In 2002 the case was appealed to the Sixth Circuit Court of Appeals, which overturned the lower court's decision. The case was then appealed to the U.S. Supreme Court in 2003, which ruled that the school's affirmative action policy could remain in place, upholding the case of Regents of the University of California v. Bakke permitting race to be a factor in admissions but banning quotas.

U.S. Government

Principles of the Constitution

The six basic principles of the Constitution are:

1. **Popular Sovereignty** – The people establish government and give power to it; the government can function only with the consent of the people.
2. **Limited Government** – The Constitution specifies limits on government authority, and no official or entity is above the law.
3. **Separation of Powers** – Power is divided among three government branches: the legislative (Congress), the executive (President), and the judicial (federal courts).
4. **Checks and Balances** – This is a system that enforces the separation of powers and ensures that each branch has the authority and ability to restrain the powers of the other two branches, thus preventing tyranny.

5. **Judicial Review** – Judges in the federal courts ensure that no act of government is in violation of the Constitution. If an act is unconstitutional, the judicial branch has the power to nullify it.
6. **Federalism** – This is the division of power between the central government and local governments, which limits the power of the federal government and allows states to deal with local problems.

Classic Forms of Government

Forms of government that have appeared throughout history include:

- **Feudalism** – This is based on the rule of local lords who are loyal to the king and control the lives and production of those who work on their land.
- **Classical republic** – This form is a representative democracy. Small groups of elected leaders represent the interests of the electorate.
- **Absolute monarchy** – A king or queen has complete control of the military and government.
- **Authoritarianism** – An individual or group has unlimited authority. There is no system in place to restrain the power of the government.
- **Dictatorship** – Those in power are not held responsible to the people.
- **Autocracy** – This is rule by one person (despot), not necessarily a monarch, who uses power tyrannically.
- **Oligarchy** – A small, usually self-appointed elite rules a region.
- **Liberal democracy** – This is a government based on the consent of the people that protects individual rights and freedoms from any intolerance by the majority.
- **Totalitarianism** – All facets of the citizens' lives are controlled by the government.

Influences of Philosophers on Political Study

Ancient Greek philosophers **Aristotle** and **Plato** believed political science would lead to order in political matters, and that this scientifically organized order would create stable, just societies.

Thomas Aquinas adapted the ideas of Aristotle to a Christian perspective. His ideas stated that individuals should have certain rights, but also certain duties, and that these rights and duties should determine the type and extent of government rule. In stating that laws should limit the role of government, he laid the groundwork for ideas that would eventually become modern constitutionalism. **Niccolò Machiavelli**, author of *The Prince*, was a proponent of politics based solely on power.

Parliamentary and Democratic Systems of Government

In a **parliamentary system**, government involves a legislature and a variety of political parties. The head of government, usually a Prime Minister, is typically the head of the dominant party. A head of state can be elected, or this position can be taken by a monarch, such as in Great Britain's constitutional monarchy system.

In a **democratic system** of government, the people elect their government representatives. The term democracy is a Greek term that means "for the rule of the people." There are two forms of democracy—direct and indirect. In a direct democracy, each issue or election is decided by a vote where each individual is counted separately. An indirect democracy employs a legislature that votes on issues that affect large number of people whom the legislative members represent.

Democracy can exist as a Parliamentary system or a Presidential system. The US is a presidential, indirect democracy.

Bill of Rights

The **United States Bill of Rights** was based on principles established by the **Magna Carta** in 1215, the 1688 **English Bill of Rights**, and the 1776 **Virginia Bill of Rights**. In 1791, the federal government added 10 amendments to the United States Constitution that provided the following **protections**:

- Freedom of speech, religion, peaceful assembly, petition of the government, and petition of the press
- The right to keep and bear arms
- No quartering of soldiers on private property without the consent of the owner
- Regulations on government search and seizure
- Provisions concerning prosecution
- The right to a speedy, public trial and the calling of witnesses
- The right to trial by jury
- Freedom from excessive bail or cruel punishment
- These rights are not necessarily the only rights
- Powers not prohibited by the Constitution are reserved to the states.

Review Video: Bill of Rights
Visit mometrix.com/academy and enter code: 585149

Making a Formal Amendment to the Constitution

So far, there have been only **27 amendments** to the federal Constitution. There are four different ways to change the wording of the constitution: two methods for proposal and two methods for ratification:

1. An amendment is proposed by a two-thirds vote in each house of Congress and ratified by three-fourths of the state legislatures.
2. An amendment is proposed by a two-thirds vote in each house of Congress and ratified by three-fourths of the states in special conventions called for that purpose.
3. An amendment is proposed by a national convention that is called by Congress at the request of two-thirds of the state legislatures and ratified by three-fourths of the state legislatures.
4. An amendment is proposed by a national convention that is called by Congress at the request of two-thirds of the state legislatures and ratified by three-fourths of the states in special conventions called for that purpose.

Review Video: Amending the Constitution
Visit mometrix.com/academy and enter code: 147023

Division of Powers

The division of powers in the federal government system is as follows:

- **National** – This level can coin money, regulate interstate and foreign trade, raise and maintain armed forces, declare war, govern United States territories and admit new states, and conduct foreign relations.
- **Concurrent** – This level can levy and collect taxes, borrow money, establish courts, define crimes and set punishments, and claim private property for public use.
- **State** – This level can regulate trade and business within the state, establish public schools, pass license requirements for professionals, regulate alcoholic beverages, conduct elections, and establish local governments.

There are three types of delegated powers granted by the Constitution:

1. **Expressed or enumerated powers** – These are specifically spelled out in the Constitution.
2. **Implied** – These are not expressly stated, but are reasonably suggested by the expressed powers.
3. **Inherent** – These are powers not expressed by the Constitution but ones that national governments have historically possessed, such as granting diplomatic recognition.

Powers can also be classified or reserved or exclusive. **Reserved powers** are not granted to the national government, but not denied to the states. **Exclusive powers** are those reserved to the national government, including concurrent powers.

Stages of Extending Suffrage in US

Originally, the Constitution of 1789 provided the right to vote only to white male property owners. Through the years, suffrage was extended through the following five stages.

1. In the early 1800s, states began to eliminate **property ownership** and **tax payment qualifications**.
2. By 1810, there were no more **religious tests** for voting. In the late 1800s, the 15th Amendment protected citizens from being denied the right to vote because of **race or color**.
3. In 1920, the 19th Amendment prohibited the denial of the right to vote because of **gender**, and women were given the right to vote.
4. Passed in 1961 and ratified in 1964, the 23rd Amendment added the voters of the **District of Columbia** to the presidential electorate and eliminated the poll tax as a condition for voting in federal elections. The **Voting Rights Act of 1965** prohibited disenfranchisement through literacy tests and various other means of discrimination.
5. In 1971, the 26th Amendment set the minimum voting age at **18 years of age**.

Major Supreme Court Cases

Out of the many Supreme Court rulings, several have had critical historical importance. These include:

- **Marbury v. Madison** (1803) – This ruling established judicial review as a power of the Supreme Court.
- **Dred Scott v. Sandford** (1857) – This decision upheld property rights over human rights in the case of a slave who had been transported to a free state by his master, but was still considered a slave.

- **Brown v. Board of Education** (1954) – The Court ruled that segregation was a violation of the Equal Protection Clause and that the "separate but equal" practice in education was unconstitutional. This decision overturned the 1896 Plessy v. Ferguson ruling that permitted segregation if facilities were equal.
- **Miranda v. Arizona** (1966) – This ruling made the reading of Miranda rights to those arrested for crimes the law. It ensured that confessions could not be illegally obtained and that citizen rights to fair trials and protection under the law would be upheld.

> **Review Video: Landmark Supreme Court Cases**
> Visit mometrix.com/academy and enter code: 753011

Famous Speeches in US History That Defined Government Policy, Foreign Relations, and American Spirit

Among the best-known speeches and famous lines known to modern Americans are the following:

- The **Gettysburg Address** – Made by Abraham Lincoln on November 19, 1863, it dedicated the battleground's cemetery.
- The **Fourteen Points** – Made by Woodrow Wilson on January 18, 1918, this outlined Wilson's plans for peace and the League of Nations.
- **Address to Congress** – Made by Franklin Roosevelt on December 8, 1941, it declared war on Japan and described the attack on Pearl Harbor as "a day which will live in infamy."
- **Inaugural Address** – Made by John F. Kennedy on January 20, 1961, it contained the famous line: "Ask not what your country can do for you, ask what you can do for your country."
- **Berlin Address** – Made by John F. Kennedy on June 26, 1963, it contained the famous line "Ich bin ein Berliner," which expressed empathy for West Berliners in their conflict with the Soviet Union.
- **"I Have a Dream"** and **"I See the Promised Land"** – Made by Martin Luther King, Jr. on August 28, 1963 and April 3, 1968, respectively, these speeches were hallmarks of the Civil Rights Movement.
- **Brandenburg Gate speech** – Made by Ronald Reagan on June 12, 1987, this speech was about the Berlin Wall and the end of the Cold War. It contained the famous line "Tear down this wall."

Closed and Open Primaries in a Direct Primary System

The **direct primary system** is a means for members of a political party to participate in the selection of a candidate from their party to compete against the other party's candidate in a general election. A **closed primary** is a party nominating election in which only declared party members can vote. Party membership is usually established by registration. Currently, 26 states and the District of Columbia use this system. An **open primary** is a party nominating election in which any qualified voter can take part. The voter makes a public choice at the polling place about which primary to participate in, and the choice does not depend on any registration or previous choices. A **blanket primary**, which allowed voters to vote in the primaries of both parties, was used at various times by three states. The Supreme Court ruled against this practice in 2000.

Important Documents in United States History and Government

The following are among the greatest **American documents** because of their impact on foreign and domestic policy:

- Declaration of Independence (1776)
- The Articles of Confederation (1777)
- The Constitution (1787) and the Bill of Rights (1791)
- The Northwest Ordinance (1787)
- The Federalist Papers (1787-88)
- George Washington's Inaugural Address (1789) and Farewell Address (1796)
- The Alien and Sedition Act (1798)
- The Louisiana Purchase Treaty (1803)
- The Monroe Doctrine (1823); The Missouri Compromise (1830)
- The Compromise of 1850
- The Kansas-Nebraska Act (1854)
- The Homestead Act (1862)
- The Emancipation Proclamation (1863)
- The agreement to purchase Alaska (1866)
- The Sherman Anti-Trust Act (1890)
- Theodore Roosevelt's Corollary to the Monroe Doctrine (1905)
- The Social Security Act (1935) and other acts of the New Deal in the 1930s; The Truman Doctrine (1947); The Marshall Plan (1948)
- The Civil Rights Act (1964)

Federal Taxes

The four types of **federal taxes** are:

- **Income taxes on individuals** – This is a complex system because of demands for various exemptions and rates. Further, the schedule of rates can be lowered or raised according to economic conditions in order to stimulate or restrain economic activity. For example, a tax cut can provide an economic stimulus, while a tax increase can slow down the rate of inflation. Personal income tax generates about five times as much as corporate taxes. Rates are based on an individual's income, and range from 10 to 35 percent.
- **Income taxes on corporations** – The same complexity of exemptions and rates exists for corporations as individuals. Taxes can be raised or lowered according to the need to stimulate or restrain the economy.
- **Excise taxes** – These are taxes on specific goods such as tobacco, liquor, automobiles, gasoline, air travel, and luxury items, or on activities such as highway usage by trucks.
- **Customs duties** – These are taxes imposed on imported goods. They serve to regulate trade between the United States and other countries.

United States Currency System

The Constitution of 1787 gave the United States Congress the central authority to **print or coin money** and to **regulate its value**. Before this time, states were permitted to maintain separate currencies. The currency system is based on a **modified gold standard**. There is an enormous store of gold to back up United States currency housed at Fort Knox, Kentucky. Paper money is actually **Federal Reserve notes** and coins. It is the job of the Bureau of Engraving and Printing in the Treasury Department to design plates, special types of paper, and other security measures for bills and bonds. This money is put into general circulation by the Treasury and Federal Reserve Banks, and is taken out of circulation when worn out. Coins are made at the Bureau of the Mint in Philadelphia, Denver, and San Francisco.

Employment Act of 1946

The **Employment Act of 1946** established the following entities to combat unemployment:

- The **Council of Economic Advisers** (CEA) – Composed of a chair and two other members appointed by the President and approved by the Senate, this council assists the President with the development and implementation of U.S. economic policy. The Council members and their staff, located in the Executive Office, are professionals in economics and statistics who forecast economic trends and provide analysis based on evidence-based research.
- The **Economic Report of the President** – This is presented every January by the President to Congress. Based on the work of the Council, the report recommends a program for maximizing employment, and may also recommend legislation.
- **Joint Economic Committee** (JEC) – This is a committee composed of 10 members of the House and 10 members of the Senate that makes a report early each year on its continuous study of the economy. Study is conducted through hearings and research, and the report is made in response to the president's recommendations.

Qualifications of a US Citizen

Anyone born in the US, born abroad to a US citizen, or who has gone through a process of **naturalization** to become a citizen, is considered a **citizen** of the United States. It is possible to lose US citizenship as a result of conviction of certain crimes such as treason. Citizenship may also be lost if a citizen pledges an oath to another country or serves in the military of a country engaged in hostilities with the US. A US citizen can also choose to hold dual citizenship, work as an expatriate in another country without losing US citizenship, or even renounce citizenship if he or she so chooses.

Rights, Duties, and Responsibilities Granted to or Expected from US Citizens

Citizens are granted certain rights under the US government. The most important of these are defined in the **Bill of Rights**, and include freedom of speech, religion, assembly, and a variety of other rights the government is not allowed to remove.

Duties of a US citizen include:

- Paying taxes
- Loyalty to the government, though the US does not prosecute those who criticize or seek to change the government
- Support and defend the Constitution
- Serve in the Armed Forces as required by law
- Obeying laws as set forth by the various levels of government.

Responsibilities of a US citizen include:

- Voting in elections
- Respecting one another's rights and not infringing upon them
- Staying informed about various political and national issues
- Respecting one another's beliefs

Representative Democracy

In a system of government characterized as a representative democracy, voters elect **representatives** to act in their interests. Typically, a representative is elected by and responsible to a specific subset of the total population of eligible voters; this subset of the electorate is referred to as a representative's constituency. A **representative democracy** may foster a more powerful legislature than other forms of government systems; to compensate for a strong legislature, most constitutions stipulate that measures must be taken to balance the powers within government, such as the creation of a separate judicial branch. Representative democracy became popular in post-industrial nations where increasing numbers of people expressed an interest in politics, but where technology and census counts remained incompatible with systems of direct democracy. Today, the majority of the world's population resides in representative democracies, including constitutional monarchies that possess a strong representative branch.

Democracy

Democracy, or rule by the people, is a form of government in which power is vested in the people and in which policy decisions are made by the majority in a decision-making process such as an election that is open to all or most citizens. Definitions of democracy have become more generalized and include aspects of society and political culture in democratic societies that do not necessarily represent a form of government. What defines a democracy varies, but some of the characteristics of a democracy could include the presence of a middle class, the presence of a civil society, a free market, political pluralism, universal suffrage, and specific rights and freedoms. In practice however, democracies do have limits on specific freedoms, which are justified as being necessary to maintain democracy and ensure democratic freedoms. For example, freedom of association is limited in democracies for individuals and groups that pose a threat to government or to society.

Presidential/Congressional System

In a **presidential system**, also referred to as a **congressional system**, the legislative branch and the executive branches are elected separately from one another. The features of a presidential system include a *president* who serves as both the head of state and the head of the government, who has no formal relationship with the legislative branch, who is not a voting member, who cannot introduce bills, and who has a fixed term of office. *Elections* are held at scheduled times. The president's *cabinet* carries out the policies of the executive branch and the legislative branch.

Political Parties

A **political party** is an organization that advocates a particular ideology and seeks to gain power within government. The tendency of members of political parties to support their party's policies and interests relative to those of other parties is referred to as partisanship. Often, a political party is comprised of members whose positions, interests and perspectives on policies vary, despite having shared interests in the general ideology of the party. As such, many political parties will have divisions within them that have differing opinions on policy. Political parties are often placed on a political spectrum, with one end of the spectrum representing conservative, traditional values and policies and the other end of the spectrum representing radical, progressive value and policies.

Review Video: Political Parties
Visit mometrix.com/academy and enter code: 640197

54

money for the purpose of supporting or opposing federal candidates, but they are allowed to spend soft money, up to a limit of $10,000 per source, on voter registration and on efforts aimed at increasing voter participation. All party committees are required to register themselves and file disclosure reports with the Federal Election Committee once their federal election activities exceed specified monetary limits.

Public Opinion

Public opinion represents the collective attitudes of individual members of the adult population in the United States of America. There are many varied forces that may influence public opinion. These forces include *public relations efforts* on the part of political campaigns and political parties. Another force affecting political opinion is the *political media* and the *mass media*. Public opinion is very important during elections, particularly Presidential elections, as it is an indicator of how candidates are perceived by the public and of how well candidates are doing during their election campaigns. Public opinion is often measured and evaluated using survey sampling.

Mass Media and Public Opinion

The **mass media** is critical in developing public opinion. In the short term people generally evaluate information they receive relative to their own beliefs; in the long term the media may have a considerable impact on people's beliefs. Due to the impact of the media on an individual's beliefs, some experts consider the effects of the media on an individual's independence and autonomy to be negative. Others view the impact of the media on individuals as a positive one, because the media provides information that expands worldviews and enriches life, and fosters the development of opinions that are informed by many sources of information. A critical aspect of the relationship between the media and public opinion is who is in control of the knowledge and information that is disseminated through the media. Whoever controls the media can propagate their own agenda. The extent to which an individual interprets and evaluates information received through the media can influence behaviors such as voting patterns or consumer behavior, as well as social attitudes.

Economics

Effects Economy Can Have on Purchasing Decisions of Consumers

The **economy** plays an important role in how careful consumers are when using their resources and what they perceive as needs as opposed to what they perceive as wants. When the economy is doing well, unemployment figures are low, which means that people can easily attain their basic necessities. As a result, consumers are typically more willing to spend their financial resources. Consumers will also be more willing to spend their resources on products and services that are not necessary to their survival, but are instead products and services that consumers enjoy having and believe increase their quality of life. On the other hand, when the economy is in a slump, consumers are much more likely to cut back on their spending because they perceive a significantly higher risk of being unable to acquire basic necessities due to a lack of financial resources.

Supply and Demand, Scarcity and Choice, and Money and Resources

Supply is the amount of a product or service available to consumers. **Demand** is how much consumers are willing to pay for the product or service. These two facets of the market determine the price of goods and services. The higher the demand, the higher the price the supplier will charge; the lower the demand, the lower the price.

Scarcity is a measure of supply in that demand is high when there is a scarcity, or low supply, of an item. **Choice** is related to scarcity and demand in that when an item in demand is scarce, consumers have to make difficult choices. They can pay more for an item, go without it, or go elsewhere for the item.

Money is the cash or currency available for payment. **Resources** are the items one can barter in exchange for goods. Money is also the cash reserves of a nation, while resources are the minerals, labor force, armaments, and other raw materials or assets a nation has available for trade.

Effects of Economic Downturn or Recession

When a **recession** happens, people at all levels of society feel the economic effects. For example:

- High **unemployment** results because businesses have to cut back to keep costs low, and may no longer have the work for the labor force they once did.
- **Mortgage rates** go up on variable-rate loans as banks try to increase their revenues, but the higher rates cause some people who cannot afford increased housing costs to sell or suffer foreclosure.
- **Credit** becomes less available as banks try to lessen their risk. This decreased lending affects business operations, home and auto loans, etc.
- **Stock market prices** drop, and the lower dividends paid to stockholders reduce their income. This is especially hard on retired people who rely on stock dividends.
- **Psychological depression and trauma** may occur in those who suffer bankruptcy, unemployment, or foreclosure during a depression.

Positive and Negative Economic Effects of Abundant Natural Resources

The **positive economic aspects** of abundant natural resources are an increase in **revenue and new jobs** where those resources have not been previously accessed. For example, the growing demand for oil, gas, and minerals has led companies to venture into new regions.

The **negative economic aspects** of abundant natural resources are:

- **Environmental degradation**, if sufficient regulations are not in place to counter strip mining, deforestation, and contamination.
- **Corruption**, if sufficient regulations are not in place to counter bribery, political favoritism, and exploitation of workers as greedy companies try to maximize their profits.
- **Social tension**, if the resources are privately owned such that the rich become richer and the poor do not reap the benefits of their national resources. Class divisions become wider, resulting in social unrest.
- **Dependence**, if the income from the natural resources is not used to develop other industries as well. In this situation, the economy becomes dependent on one source, and faces potential crises if natural disasters or depletion take away that income source.

Economics and Kinds of Economies

Economics is the study of the buying choices that people make, the production of goods and services, and how our market system works. The two kinds of economies are command and market. In a **command economy**, the government controls what and how much is produced, the methods used for production, and the distribution of goods and services. In a market economy, producers make decisions about methods and distribution on their own. These choices are based on what will sell and bring a profit in the marketplace. In a **market economy**, consumers ultimately affect these decisions by choosing whether or not to buy certain goods and services. The United States has a market economy.

Market Economy

The five characteristics of a **market economy** are:

- **Economic freedom** – There is freedom of choice with respect to jobs, salaries, production, and price.
- **Economic incentives** – A positive incentive is to make a profit. However, if the producer tries to make too high a profit, the consequences might be that no one will purchase the item at that price. A negative incentive would be a drop in profits, causing the producer to decrease or discontinue production. A boycott, which might cause the producer to change business practices or policies, is also a negative economic incentive.
- **Competition** – There is more than one producer for any given product. Consumers thereby have choices about what to buy, which are usually made based on quality and price. Competition is an incentive for a producer to make the best product at the best price. Otherwise, producers will lose business to the competition.
- **Private ownership** – Production and profits belong to an individual or to a private company, not to the government.
- **Limited government** – Government plays no role in the economic decisions of its individual citizens.

Factors of Production and Types of Markets That Create Economic Flow

The factors of **production** are:

- **Land** – This includes not only actual land, but also forests, minerals, water, etc.
- **Labor** – This is the work force required to produce goods and services, including factors such as talent, skills, and physical labor.
- **Capital** – This is the cash and material equipment needed to produce goods and services, including buildings, property, tools, office equipment, roads, etc.
- **Entrepreneurship** – Persons with initiative can capitalize on the free market system by producing goods and services.

The two types of markets are factor and product markets. The **factor market** consists of the people who exchange their services for wages. The people are sellers and companies are buyers. The **product market** is the selling of products to the people who want to buy them. The people are the buyers and the companies are the sellers. This exchange creates a circular economic flow in which money goes from the producers to workers as wages, and then flows back to producers in the form of payment for products.

Economic Impact of Technology

At the start of the 21st century, the role of **information and communications technologies** (ICT) grew rapidly as the economy shifted to a knowledge-based one. Output is increasing in areas where ICT is used intensively, which are service areas and knowledge-intensive industries such as finance; insurance; real estate; business services, health care, and environmental goods and services; and community, social, and personal services. Meanwhile, the economic share for manufacturers is declining in medium- and low-technology industries such as chemicals, food products, textiles, gas, water, electricity, construction, and transport and communication services. Industries that have traditionally been high-tech, such as aerospace, computers, electronics, and pharmaceuticals are remaining steady in terms of their economic share. Technology has become the strongest factor in determining **per capita income** for many countries. The ease of technology investments as compared to industries that involve factories and large labor forces has resulted in more foreign investments in countries that do not have natural resources to call upon.

U.S. and World History

U.S. History

Contributions of Early French Explorers

The **French** never succeeded in attracting settlers to their territories. Those who came were more interested in the fur and fish trades than in forming colonies. Eventually, the French ceded their southern possessions and New Orleans, founded in 1718, to Spain. However, the French made major contributions to the exploration of the new continent, including:

- **Giovanni da Verrazano** and **Jacques Cartier** explored the North American coast and the St. Lawrence Seaway for France.
- **Samuel de Champlain**, who founded Quebec and set up a fur empire on the St. Lawrence Seaway, also explored the coasts of Massachusetts and Rhode Island between 1604 and 1607.
- **Fr. Jacques Marquette**, a Jesuit missionary, and **Louis Joliet** were the first Europeans to travel down the Mississippi in 1673.
- **Rene-Robert de la Salle** explored the Great Lakes and the Illinois and Mississippi Rivers from 1679-1682, claiming all the land from the Great Lakes to the Gulf of Mexico and from the Appalachians to the Rockies for France.

Earliest Spanish Explorers

The **Spanish** claimed and explored huge portions of the United States after the voyages of Christopher Columbus. Among them were:

- **Juan Ponce de Leon** – In 1513, he became the first European in Florida; established the oldest European settlement in Puerto Rico; discovered the Gulf Stream; and searched for the fountain of youth.
- **Alonso Alvarez de Pineda** – He charted the Gulf Coast from Florida to Mexico in 1519. Probably the first European in Texas, he claimed it for Spain.
- **Panfilo de Narvaez** – He docked in Tampa Bay with Cabeza de Vaca in 1528, claimed Florida for Spain, and then sailed the Gulf Coast.
- **Alvar Nuñez Cabeza de Vaca** – He got lost on foot in Texas and New Mexico. Estevanico, or Esteban, a Moorish slave, was a companion who guided them to Mexico.
- **Francisco Vásquez de Coronado** – While searching for gold in 1540, he became the first European to explore Kansas, Oklahoma, Texas, New Mexico, and Arizona.
- **Hernando De Soto** – He was the first European to explore the southeastern United States from Tallahassee to Natchez.

Colonization of Virginia and the Virginia Company

In 1585, **Sir Walter Raleigh** landed on Roanoke Island and sent Arthur Barlow to the mainland, which they named **Virginia**. Two attempts to establish settlements failed. The first permanent English colony was founded by Captain John Smith in **Jamestown** in 1607. The **Virginia Company** and the **Chesapeake Bay Company** successfully colonized other Virginia sites. By 1619, Virginia had a House of Burgesses. The crown was indifferent to the colony, so local government grew strong and tobacco created wealth. The First Families of Virginia dominated politics there for two centuries, and four of the first five United States presidents came from these families. The Virginia

Company sent 24 Puritan families, known as **Pilgrims**, to Virginia on the **Mayflower**. In 1620, it landed at Plymouth, Massachusetts instead. The **Plymouth Plantation** was established and survived with the help of natives. This is where the first Thanksgiving is believed to have occurred.

Colonization in Massachusetts, Maryland, Rhode Island, and Pennsylvania

In 1629, 400 Puritans arrived in **Salem**, which became an important port and was made famous by the witch trials in 1692. In 1628, the self-governed **Massachusetts Bay Company** was organized, and the Massachusetts Indians sold most of the land to the English. **Boston** was established in 1630 and **Harvard University** was established in 1636.

Maryland was established by Lord Baltimore in 1632 in the hopes of providing refuge for English Catholics. The Protestant majority, however, opposed this religious tolerance.

Roger Williams was banished from Massachusetts in 1636 because he called for separation of church and state. He established the **Rhode Island** colony in 1647 and had 800 settlers by 1650, including Anne Hutchinson and her "Antinomians," who attacked clerical authority.

In 1681, **William Penn** received a royal charter for the establishment of **Pennsylvania** as a colony for Quakers. However, religious tolerance allowed immigrants from a mixed group of denominations, who prospered from the beginning.

Reasons for American Revolution

The English colonies **rebelled** for the following reasons:

- England was remote yet **controlling**. By 1775, few Americans had ever been to England. They considered themselves Americans, not English.
- During the Seven Years' War (aka French and Indian War) from 1754-1763, Americans, including George Washington, served in the British army, but were treated as **inferiors**.
- It was feared that the Anglican Church might try to expand in the colonies and **inhibit religious freedom**.
- Heavy **taxation** such as the Sugar and Stamp Acts, which were created solely to create revenue for the crown, and business controls such as restricting trade of certain products to England only, were burdensome.
- The colonies had no official **representation** in the English Parliament and wanted to govern themselves.
- There were fears that Britain would block westward expansion and independent enterprise.
- **Local government**, established through elections by property holders, was already functioning.

Important Events and Groups Leading up to American Revolution

Over several years, various events and groups contributed to the rebellion that became a revolution:

- **Sons of Liberty** – This was the protest group headed by Samuel Adams that incited the Revolution.
- **Boston Massacre** – On March 5, 1770, soldiers fired on a crowd and killed five people.
- **Committees of Correspondence** – These were set up throughout the colonies to transmit revolutionary ideas and create a unified response.

Andrew Jackson Presidency

A number of important milestones occurred in American history during the presidency of **Andrew Jackson**. They included:

- Jackson's election is considered the beginning of the modern political party system and the start of the **Democratic Party**.
- Jeffersonian Democracy, a system governed by middle and upper class educated property holders, was replaced by **Jacksonian Democracy**, a system that allowed universal white male suffrage.
- The **Indian Removal Act of 1830** took natives out of territories that whites wanted to settle, most notably the Trail of Tears that removed Cherokees from Georgia and relocated them to Oklahoma.
- The issue of **nullification**, the right of states to nullify any federal laws they thought unconstitutional, came to a head over tariffs. However, a strong majority vote in Congress supporting the Tariff Acts cemented the policy that states must comply with federal laws.

Whig Party

The **Whig Party** existed from 1833 to 1856. It started in opposition to Jackson's **authoritarian policies** and was particularly concerned with defending the supremacy of Congress over the executive branch, states' rights, economic protectionism, and modernization. Notable members included: Daniel Webster, Henry Clay, Winfield Scott, and a young Abraham Lincoln. The Whigs had four presidents: William Henry Harrison, Zachary Taylor, John Tyler (expelled from the party), and Millard Fillmore. However, the Whigs won only two presidential elections. Harrison and Taylor were elected in 1840 and 1848, respectively. However, both died in office, so Tyler and Fillmore assumed the presidency. In 1852, the anti-slavery faction of the party kept Fillmore from getting the nomination. Instead, it went to Scott, who was soundly defeated. In 1856, the Whigs supported Fillmore and the National American Party, but lost badly. Thereafter, the **split over slavery** caused the party to dissolve.

Important 19th Century American Writers

In the 19th century, American literature became an entity of its own and provided a distinct voice for the American experience. **James Fenimore Cooper** was a great writer from this time period. He was the first to write about Native Americans, and was the author of the Leatherstocking series, which includes *The Last of the Mohicans* and *The Deerslayer*.

- **Ralph Waldo Emerson** – He was an essayist, philosopher, and poet, and also the leader of the Transcendentalist movement. His notable works include "Self-Reliance" and "The American Scholar."

- **Nathaniel Hawthorne** – This novelist and short story writer wrote *The Scarlet Letter, The House of Seven Gables*, "Young Goodman Brown," and "The Minister's Black Veil."
- **Herman Melville** – He was a novelist, essayist, short story writer, and poet who wrote *Moby Dick, Billy Budd*, and "Bartleby the Scrivener." **Edgar Allan Poe** – He was a poet, literary critic, and master of the short story, especially horror and detective stories. His notable works include "The Tell-Tale Heart," "The Pit and the Pendulum," "Annabel Lee," and "The Raven."
- **Harriet Beecher Stowe** – She was the author of *Uncle Tom's Cabin*.
- **Henry David Thoreau** – He was a poet, naturalist, and Transcendentalist who wrote *Walden* and *Civil Disobedience*.
- **Walt Whitman** – He was a poet, essayist, and journalist who wrote *Leaves of Grass* and "O Captain! My Captain!"

19th Century Social and Religious Leaders

Some of the important social and religious leaders from the 19th century were:

- **Susan B. Anthony** – A women's rights and abolition activist, she lectured across the nation for suffrage, property and wage rights, and labor organizations for women.
- **Dorothea Dix** – She created the first American asylums for the treatment of mental illness and served as the Superintendent of Army Nurses during the War Between the States.
- **Frederick Douglass** –An escaped slave who became an abolitionist leader, government official, and writer.
- **William Lloyd Garrison** –An abolitionist and the editor of the *Liberator*, the leading anti-slavery newspaper of the time.
- **Joseph Smith** – He founded the Latter-Day Saints (Mormonism) in 1829.
- **Horace Mann** – A leader of the common school movement that made public education a right of all Americans.
- **Elizabeth Cady Stanton** – With Lucretia Mott, she held the Seneca Falls Convention in 1848, demanding women's suffrage and other reforms.
- **Brigham Young** –The leader of the Mormons when they fled religious persecution, built Salt Lake City, and settled much of the West. He was the first governor of the Utah Territory.

Compromise of 1850, Fugitive Slave Law, Kansas-Nebraska Act, Bleeding Kansas, and Dred Scott Case

- The **Compromise of 1850**, calling upon the principle of popular sovereignty, allowed those who lived in the Mexican cession to decide for themselves whether to be a free or slave territory.
- The **Fugitive Slave Law of 1850** allowed slave owners to go into free states to retrieve their escaped slaves.
- The **Kansas-Nebraska Act of 1854** repealed the Missouri Compromise of 1820 to allow the lands from the Louisiana Purchase to settle the slavery issue by popular sovereignty. Outraged Northerners responded by defecting from the Whig Party and starting the Republican Party.
- **Bleeding Kansas** was the name applied to the state when a civil war broke out between pro- and anti-slavery advocates while Kansas was trying to formalize its statutes before being admitted as a state.

- The **Dred Scott vs. Sandford case** was decided by the Supreme Court in 1857. It was ruled that Congress had no authority to exclude slavery from the territories, which in effect meant that the Missouri Compromise had been unconstitutional.

States Forming the Confederacy and Leaders of the War Between the States

The states that **seceded** from the Union to form the **Confederacy** were: Georgia, Arkansas, South Carolina, North Carolina, Virginia, Florida, Mississippi, Alabama, Louisiana, Texas, and Tennessee. The slave-holding states that were kept in the Union were Delaware, Maryland, Kentucky, and Missouri.

- **Jefferson Davis** of Mississippi, a former U. S. senator and cabinet member, was the president of the Confederacy.
- **Abraham Lincoln** of Illinois was the President of the United States. His election triggered the secession of the south. He was assassinated shortly after winning a second term.
- **Robert E. Lee** of Virginia was offered the position of commanding general of the Union Army, but declined because of loyalty to his home state. He led the Army of Northern Virginia and the central Confederate force, and is still considered a military mastermind.
- **Ulysses S. Grant** of Ohio wasn't appointed to command the Union Army until 1864, after a series of other commanders were unsuccessful. He received Lee's surrender at the Appomattox Court House in Virginia in April, 1865, and went on to become President from 1869 to 1877.

Reconstruction and 13th, 14th, and 15th Amendments

Reconstruction was the period from 1865 to 1877, during which the South was under strict control of the U.S. government. In March, 1867, all state governments of the former Confederacy were terminated, and **military occupation** began. Military commanders called for constitutional conventions to reconstruct the state governments, to which delegates were to be elected by universal male suffrage. After a state government was in operation and the state had **ratified the 14th Amendment**, its representatives were admitted to Congress. Three constitutional amendments from 1865 to 1870, which tried to rectify the problems caused by slavery, became part of the Reconstruction effort. The **13th Amendment** declared slavery illegal. The **14th Amendment** made all persons born or naturalized in the country U.S. citizens, and forbade any state to interfere with their fundamental civil rights. The **15th Amendment** made it illegal to deny individuals the right to vote on the grounds of race. In his 1876 election campaign, President **Rutherford B. Hayes** promised to withdraw the troops, and did so in 1877.

Major Changes in Industry in the Late 1800s

Important events during this time of enormous business growth and large-scale exploitation of natural resources were:

- **Industrialization** – Like the rest of the world, the United States' entry into the Industrial Age was marked by many new inventions and the mechanization of factories.
- **Railroad expansion** – The Transcontinental Railroad was built from 1865 to 1969. Railroad tracks stretched over 35,000 miles in 1865, but that distance reached 240,000 miles by 1910. The raw materials and manufactured goods needed for the railroads kept mines and factories very busy.
- **Gold and silver mining** – Mines brought many prospectors to the West from 1850 to about 1875, but mining corporations soon took over.

- **Cattle ranching** – This was a large-scale enterprise beginning in the late 1860s, but by the 1880s open ranges were being fenced and plowed for farming and pastures. Millions of farmers moved into the high plains, establishing the "Bread Basket," which was the major wheat growing area of the country.

Gilded Age and Infamous Robber Barons

The **Gilded Age**, from the 1870s to 1890, was so named because of the enormous wealth and grossly opulent lifestyle enjoyed by a handful of powerful families. This was the time when huge mansions were built as summer "cottages" in Newport, Rhode Island, and great lodges were built in mountain areas for the pleasure of families such as the Vanderbilts, Ascots, and Rockefellers. Control of the major industries was held largely by the following men, who were known as **Robber Barons** for their ruthless business practices and exploitation of workers: Jay Gould, railroads; Andrew Carnegie, steel; John D. Rockefeller, Sr., oil; Philip Danforth Armour, meatpacking; J. P. Morgan, banking; John Jacob Astor, fur pelts; and Cornelius Vanderbilt, steamboat shipping. Of course, all of these heads of industry diversified and became involved in multiple business ventures. To curb cutthroat competition, particularly among the railroads, and to prohibit restrained trade, Congress created the **Interstate Commerce Commission** and the **Sherman Anti-Trust Act**. Neither of these, however, was enforced.

> **Review Video: The Gilded Age: An Overview**
> Visit mometrix.com/academy and enter code: 684770
>
> **Review Video: The Gilded Age: Chinese Immigration**
> Visit mometrix.com/academy and enter code: 624166
>
> **Review Video: The Gilded Age: Labor Strikes**
> Visit mometrix.com/academy and enter code: 683116
>
> **Review Video: The Gilded Age: Labor Unions**
> Visit mometrix.com/academy and enter code: 749692

Immigration Trends in Late 1800s

The population of the United States doubled between 1860 and 1890, the period that saw 10 million **immigrants** arrive. Most lived in the north. Cities and their **slums** grew tremendously because of immigration and industrialization. While previous immigrants had come from Germany, Scandinavia, and Ireland, the 1880s saw a new wave of immigrants from Italy, Poland, Hungary, Bohemia, and Greece, as well as Jewish groups from central and eastern Europe, especially Russia. The Roman Catholic population grew from 1.6 million in 1850 to 12 million in 1900, a growth that ignited an anti-Catholic backlash from the anti-Catholic Know-Nothing Party of the 1880s and the Ku Klux Klan. Exploited immigrant workers started **labor protests** in the 1870s, and the **Knights of Labor** was formed in 1878, calling for sweeping social and economic reform. Its membership reached 700,000 by 1886. Eventually, this organization was replaced by the **American Federation of Labor**, headed by Samuel Gompers.

Effects of Progressive Movement on Foreign Affairs

The **Progressive Era**, which was the time period from the 1890s to the 1920s, got its name from progressive, reform-minded political leaders who wanted to export a just and rational social order to the rest of the world while increasing trade with foreign markets. Consequently, the United States interfered in a dispute between Venezuela and Britain. America invoked the **Monroe**

70

Doctrine and sided with Cuba in its independence struggle against Spain. The latter resulted in the **Spanish-American Wars** in 1898 that ended with Cuba, Puerto Rico, the Philippines, and Guam becoming American protectorates at the same time the United States annexed Hawaii. In 1900, America declared an **Open Door policy** with China to support its independence and open markets. In 1903, Theodore Roosevelt helped Panama become independent of Columbia, and then secured the right to build the **Panama Canal**. Roosevelt also negotiated the peace treaty to end the Russo-Japanese War, which earned him the Nobel Peace prize. He then sent the American fleet on a world cruise to display his country's power.

> **Review Video: The Progressive Era**
> Visit mometrix.com/academy and enter code: 722394

Domestic Accomplishments of Progressive Era

To the Progressives, promoting law and order meant cleaning up city governments to make them honest and efficient, bringing more democracy and humanity to state governments, and establishing a core of social workers to improve slum housing, health, and education. Also during the **Progressive Era**, the national government strengthened or created the following regulatory agencies, services, and acts to oversee business enterprise:

- Passed in 1906, the **Hepburn A**ct reinforced the Interstate Commerce Commission. In 1902, Roosevelt used the Justice Department and lawsuits to try to break monopolies and enforce the **Sherman Anti-Trust Act**. The **Clayton Anti-Trust Act** was added in 1914.
- From 1898 to 1910, the **Forest Service** guided lumber companies in the conservation and more efficient use of woodland resources under the direction of Gifford Pinchot.
- In 1906, the **Pure Food and Drug Act** was passed to protect consumers from fraudulent labeling and adulteration of products.
- In 1913, the **Federal Reserve System** was established to supervise banking and commerce. In 1914, the **Fair Trade Commission** was established to ensure fair competition.

US Involvement in World War I

When World War I broke out in 1914, America declared **neutrality**. The huge demand for war goods by the Allies broke a seven-year industrial stagnation and gave American factories full-time work. The country's sympathies lay mostly with the Allies, and before long American business and banking were heavily invested in an Allied victory. In 1916, **Woodrow Wilson** campaigned on the slogan "He kept us out of war." However, when the British ship the *Lusitania* was torpedoed in 1915 by a German submarine and many Americans were killed, Wilson had already warned the Germans that the United States would enter the war if Germany interfered with neutral ships at sea. Eventually, when it was proven that Germany was trying to incite Mexico and Japan into attacking the United States, Wilson declared war in 1917, even though America was unprepared.

Nonetheless, America quickly armed and transferred sufficient troops to Europe, bringing the **Allies** to victory in 1918.

> **Review Video: WWI Overview**
> Visit mometrix.com/academy and enter code: 659767
>
> **Review Video: World War I: European Alliances**
> Visit mometrix.com/academy and enter code: 257458
>
> **Review Video: World War I: Outcomes**
> Visit mometrix.com/academy and enter code: 278666

Decade of Optimism

After World War I, **Warren Harding** ran for President on the slogan "return to normalcy" and concentrated on domestic affairs. The public felt optimistic because life improved due to affordable automobiles from Henry Ford's mass production system, better roads, electric lights, airplanes, new communication systems, and voting rights for women (19th Amendment, 1920). Radio and movies helped develop a national culture. For the first time, the majority of Americans lived in **cities**. Young people shortened dresses and haircuts, and smoked and drank in public despite Prohibition (18th Amendment, 1919). Meantime, the **Russian Revolution** caused a **Red Scare** that strengthened the already strong Ku Klux Klan that controlled some states' politics. In 1925, the **Scopes trial** in Tennessee convicted a high school teacher for presenting Darwinian theories. The **Teapot Dome scandal** rocked the Harding administration. After Harding died in 1923, **Calvin Coolidge** became president. He was followed by **Herbert Hoover**, a strong proponent of capitalism under whom unregulated business led to the 1929 stock crash.

Great Depression and Dust Bowl

In the 1920s, the rich got richer. After World War I, however, farmers were in a depression when foreign markets started growing their own crops again. Increased credit buying, bank war debts, a huge gap between rich and poor, and a belief that the stock market would always go up got the nation into financial trouble. The **Stock Market Crash** in October 1929 that destroyed fortunes dramatized the downward spiral of the whole economy. Banks failed, and customers lost all their money. By 1933, 14 million were unemployed, industrial production was down to one-third of its 1929 level, and national income had dropped by half. Adding to the misery of farmers, years of breaking sod on the prairies without adequate conservation techniques caused the topsoil to fly away in great **dust storms** that blackened skies for years, causing deaths from lung disease and failed crops.

US Role in World War II

World War II began in 1939. As with World War I, the United States tried to stay out of World War II, even though the **Lend-Lease program** transferred munitions to Great Britain. However, on December 7, 1941, Japan attacked **Pearl Harbor** in Hawaii. Since Japan was an ally of Germany, the United States declared war on all the Axis powers. Although there was fighting in both Europe and the Pacific, the decision was made to concentrate on defeating Hitler first. Since it did not have combat within its borders, the United States became the great manufacturer of goods and munitions for the war effort. Women went to work in the factories, while the men entered the military. All facets of American life were centered on the war effort, including rationing, metal collections, and buying war bonds. The benefit of this production was an **end to the economic**

72

depression. The influx of American personnel and supplies eventually brought victory in Europe in April of 1945, and in Asia the following August.

> **Review Video: World War II**
> Visit mometrix.com/academy and enter code: 759402
>
> **Review Video: World War II: Germany**
> Visit mometrix.com/academy and enter code: 951452
>
> **Review Video: World War II: Japan**
> Visit mometrix.com/academy and enter code: 313104

Major Programs and Events Resulting from the Cold War

After World War II, the Soviet Union kept control of Eastern Europe, including half of Germany. **Communism** spread around the world. Resulting fears led to:

- The **Truman Doctrine** (1947) – This was a policy designed to protect free peoples everywhere against oppression.
- The **Marshall Plan** (1948) – This devoted $12 billion to rebuild Western Europe and strengthen its defenses.
- The **Organization of American States** (1948) – This was established to bolster democratic relations in the Americas.
- The **Berlin Blockade** (1948-49) – The Soviets tried to starve out West Berlin, so the United States provided massive supply drops by air.
- The **North Atlantic Treaty Organization** (1949) – This was formed to militarily link the United States and western Europe so that an attack on one was an attack on both.
- The **Korean War** (1950-53) – This divided the country into the communist North and the democratic South.
- The **McCarthy era** (1950-54) – Senator Joseph McCarthy of Wisconsin held hearings on supposed Communist conspiracies that ruined innocent reputations and led to the blacklisting of suspected sympathizers in the government, Hollywood, and the media.

> **Review Video: The Cold War: The United States and Russia**
> Visit mometrix.com/academy and enter code: 981433

Major Events of 1960s

The 1960s were a tumultuous time for the United States. Major events included:

- The **Cuban Missile Crisis** (1961) – This was a stand-off between the United States and the Soviet Union over a build-up of missiles in Cuba. Eventually, the Soviets stopped their shipments and a nuclear war was averted.
- The assassinations of President Kennedy (1963), Senator Robert Kennedy (1968), and Dr. Martin Luther King, Jr. (1968).
- The **Civil Rights Movement** – Protest marches held across the nation to draw attention to the plight of black citizens. From 1964 to 1968, race riots exploded in more than 100 cities.
- The **Vietnam War** (1964-73) – This resulted in a military draft. There was heavy involvement of American personnel and money. There were also protest demonstrations, particularly on college campuses. At Kent State, several students died after being shot by National Guardsmen.

- **Major legislation** – Legislation passed during this decade included the Civil Rights Act, the Clean Air Act, and the Water Quality Act. This decade also saw the creation of the Peace Corps, Medicare, and the War on Poverty, in which billions were appropriated for education, urban redevelopment, and public housing.

Presidents and Vice Presidents from 1972 to 1974

In a two-year time span, the United States had two presidents and two vice presidents. This situation resulted first from the resignation of Vice President **Spiro T. Agnew** in October of 1973 because of alleged kickbacks. President **Richard M. Nixon** then appointed House Minority Leader **Gerald R. Ford** to be vice president. This was accomplished through Senate ratification, a process that had been devised after Harry Truman succeeded to the presidency upon the death of Franklin Roosevelt and went through nearly four years of his presidency without a vice president. Nixon resigned the presidency in August of 1974 because some Republican party members broke into Democratic headquarters at the **Watergate** building in Washington, DC, and the president participated in covering up the crime. Ford succeeded Nixon, and had to appoint another vice president. He chose **Nelson Rockefeller**, former governor of New York.

World History

Important Contributions of Ancient Civilizations of Sumer, Egypt, and Indus Valley

These three ancient civilizations are distinguished by their unique contributions to the development of world civilization:

- **Sumer** used the first known writing system, which enabled the Sumerians to leave a sizeable written record of their myths and religion; advanced the development of the wheel and irrigation; and urbanized their culture with a cluster of cities.
- **Egypt** was united by the Nile River. Egyptians originally settled in villages on its banks; had a national religion that held their pharaohs as gods; had a central government that controlled civil and artistic affairs; and had writing and libraries.
- The **Indus Valley** was also called Harappan after the city of Harappa. This civilization started in the 3rd and 4th centuries BC and was widely dispersed over 400,000 square miles. It had a unified culture of luxury and refinement, no known national government, an advanced civic system, and prosperous trade routes.

> **Review Video: Early Mesopotamia: The Sumerians**
> Visit mometrix.com/academy and enter code: 939880
>
> **Review Video: Egyptians**
> Visit mometrix.com/academy and enter code: 398041

Common Traits and Cultural Identifiers of Early Empires of Mesopotamia, Egypt, Greece, and Rome

The common traits of these empires were: a strong military; a centralized government; control and standardization of commerce, money, and taxes; a weight system; and an official language. **Mesopotamia** had a series of short-term empires that failed because of their oppression of subject peoples. **Egypt** also had a series of governments after extending its territory beyond the Nile area. Compared to Mesopotamia, these were more stable and long-lived because they blended different peoples to create a single national identity. **Greece** started as a group of city-states that were united

74

by Alexander the Great and joined to create an empire that stretched from the Indus River to Egypt and the Mediterranean coast. Greece blended Greek values with those of the local cultures, which collectively became known as Hellenistic society. **Rome** was an Italian city-state that grew into an empire extending from the British Isles across Europe to the Middle East. It lasted for 1,000 years and became the foundation of the Western world's culture, language, and laws.

Review Video: Ancient Greece
Visit mometrix.com/academy and enter code: 800829

Major Deities of Greek and Roman Mythology

The major gods of the **Greek/Roman mythological system** are:

- **Zeus/Jupiter** – Head of the Pantheon, god of the sky
- **Hera/Juno** – Wife of Zeus/Jupiter, goddess of marriage
- **Poseidon/Neptune** – God of the seas
- **Demeter/Ceres** – Goddess of grain
- **Apollo** – God of the sun, law, music, archery, healing, and truth
- **Artemis/Diana** – Goddess of the moon, wild creatures, and hunting
- **Athena/Minerva** – Goddess of civilized life, handicrafts, and agriculture
- **Hephaestus/Vulcan** – God of fire, blacksmith
- **Aphrodite/Venus** – Goddess of love and beauty
- **Ares/Mars** – God of war
- **Dionysus/Bacchus** – God of wine and vegetation
- **Hades/Pluto** – God of the underworld and the dead
- **Eros/Cupid** – Minor god of love
- **Hestia/Vesta** – Goddess of the hearth or home
- **Hermes/Mercury** – Minor god of gracefulness and swiftness

Characteristics of Chinese and Indian Empires

While the Chinese had the world's longest lasting and continuous empires, the Indians had more of a cohesive culture than an empire system. Their distinct characteristics are as follows:

- **China** – Since the end of the Warring States period in 221 BC, China has functioned as an empire. Although the dynasties changed several times, the basic governmental structure remained the same into the 20th century. The Chinese also have an extensive written record of their culture which heavily emphasizes history, philosophy, and a common religion.
- **India** – The subcontinent was seldom unified in terms of government until the British empire controlled the area in the 19th and 20th centuries. In terms of culture, India has had persistent institutions and religions that have loosely united the people, such as the caste system and guilds. These have regulated daily life more than any government.

Middle Ages in European History

The **Middle Ages**, or Medieval times, was a period that ran from approximately 500-1500 AD. During this time, the centers of European civilization moved from the Mediterranean countries to

France, Germany, and England, where strong national governments were developing. Key events of this time include:

- **Roman Catholicism** was the cultural and religious center of medieval life, extending into politics and economics.
- **Knights**, with their systems of honor, combat, and chivalry, were loyal to their king. **Peasants**, or serfs, served a particular lord and his lands.
- Many **universities** were established that still function in modern times.
- The **Crusades**, the recurring wars between European Christians and Middle East Muslims, raged over the Holy Lands.
- One of the legendary leaders was Charles the Great, or **Charlemagne**, who created an empire across France and Germany around 800 AD.
- The **Black Death plague** swept across Europe from 1347-1350, leaving between one third and one half of the population dead.

> **Review Video: The Middle Ages**
> Visit mometrix.com/academy and enter code: 413133

Protestant Reformation

The dominance of the **Catholic Church** during the Middle Ages in Europe gave it immense power, which encouraged corrupt practices such as the selling of indulgences and clerical positions. The **Protestant Reformation** began as an attempt to reform the Catholic Church, but eventually led to the separation from it. In 1517, Martin Luther posted his *Ninety-Five Theses* on the door of a church in Saxony, which criticized unethical practices, various doctrines, and the authority of the pope. Other reformers such as John Calvin and John Wesley soon followed, but disagreed among themselves and divided along doctrinal lines. Consequently, the Lutheran, Reformed, Calvinist, and Presbyterian churches were founded, among others. In England, King Henry VIII was denied a divorce by the pope, so he broke away and established the **Anglican Church**. The Protestant reformation caused the Catholic Church to finally reform itself, but the Protestant movement continued, resulting in a proliferation of new denominations.

Renaissance

Renaissance is the French word for rebirth, and is used to describe the renewal of interest in ancient Greek and Latin art, literature, and philosophy that occurred in Europe, especially Italy, from the 14th through the 16th centuries. Historically, it was also a time of great scientific inquiry, the rise of individualism, extensive geographical exploration, and the rise of secular values.

Notable figures of the Renaissance include:

- **Petrarch** – An Italian scholar, writer, and key figure in northern Italy, which is where the Renaissance started and where chief patrons came from the merchant class
- **Leonardo da Vinci** – Artist and inventor
- Michelangelo and Raphael – Artists
- **Desiderius Erasmus** – Applied historical scholarship to the New Testament and laid the seeds for the Protestant Reformation
- **Sir Thomas More** – A lawyer and author who wrote *Utopia*
- **Niccolò Machiavelli** – Author of *Prince and Discourses*, which proposed a science of human nature and civil life
- **William Shakespeare** – A renowned playwright and poet

Industrial Revolution

The **Industrial Revolution** started in England with the construction of the first **cotton mill** in 1733. Other inventions and factories followed in rapid succession. The **steel industry** grew exponentially when it was realized that cheap, abundant English coal could be used instead of wood for melting metals. The **steam engine**, which revolutionized transportation and work power, came next. Around 1830, a factory-based, **technological era** was ushered into the rest of Europe. Society changed from agrarian to urban. A need for cheap, unskilled labor resulted in the extensive employment and abuse of women and children, who worked up to 14 hours a day, six days a week in deplorable conditions. Expanding populations brought crowded, unsanitary conditions to the cities, and the factories created air and water pollution. Societies had to deal with these new situations by enacting **child labor laws** and creating **labor unions** to protect the safety of workers.

Participants of World War I and World War II

World War I, which began in 1914, was fought by the **Allies** Britain, France, Russia, Greece, Italy, Romania, and Serbia. They fought against the **Central Powers** of Germany, Austria-Hungary, Bulgaria, and Turkey. In 1917, the United States joined the Allies, and Russia withdrew to pursue its own revolution. World War I ended in 1918.

World War II was truly a world war, with fighting occurring on nearly every continent. Germany occupied most of Europe and Northern Africa. It was opposed by the countries of the British Empire, free France and its colonies, Russia, and various national resistance forces. Japan, an **Axis** ally of Germany, had been forcefully expanding its territories in Korea, China, Indonesia, the Philippines, and the South Pacific for many years. When Japan attacked Pearl Harbor in 1941, the United States joined the **Allied** effort. Italy changed from the Axis to the Allied side mid-war after deposing its own dictator. The war ended in Europe in April 1945, and in Japan in August 1945.

Importance of Cross-Cultural Comparisons in World History Instruction

It is important to make **cross-cultural comparisons** when studying world history so that the subject is **holistic** and not oriented to just Western civilization. Not only are the contributions of civilizations around the world important, but they are also interesting and more representative of the mix of cultures present in the United States. It is also critical to the understanding of world relations to study the involvement of European countries and the United States in international commerce, colonization, and development. **Trade routes** from ancient times linked Africa, Asia, and Europe, resulting in exchanges and migrations of people, philosophies, and religions, as well as goods. While many civilizations in the Americas thrived and some became very sophisticated, many eventually became disastrously entangled in **European expansion**. The historic isolation of China and the modern industrialization of Japan have had huge impacts on relations with the rest of the world. The more students understand this history and its effects on the modern world, the better they will able to function in their own spheres.

Geography and Social Studies Concepts

Geography

Important Terms Related to Maps

The most important terms used when describing items on a map or globe are:

- **Latitude and longitude** – Latitude and longitude are the imaginary lines (horizontal and vertical, respectively) that divide the globe into a grid. Both are measured using the 360 degrees of a circle.
- **Coordinates** – These are the latitude and longitude measures for a place.
- **Absolute location** – This is the exact spot where coordinates meet. The grid system allows the location of every place on the planet to be identified.
- **Equator** – This is the line at 0° latitude that divides the earth into two equal halves called hemispheres.
- **Parallels** – This is another name for lines of latitude because they circle the earth in parallel lines that never meet.
- **Meridians** – This is another name for lines of longitude. The Prime Meridian is located at 0° longitude, and is the starting point for measuring distance (both east and west) around the globe. Meridians circle the earth and connect at the Poles.

> **Review Video: 5 Elements of any Map**
> Visit mometrix.com/academy and enter code: 437727

Four Hemispheres, North and South Poles, Tropics of Cancer and Capricorn, and Arctic and Antarctic Circles

The definitions for these terms are as follows:

- **Northern Hemisphere** – This is the area above, or north, of the equator.
- **Southern Hemisphere** – This is the area below, or south, of the equator.
- **Western Hemisphere** – This is the area between the North and South Poles. It extends west from the Prime Meridian to the International Date Line.
- **Eastern Hemisphere** – This is the area between the North and South Poles. It extends east from the Prime Meridian to the International Date Line.
- **North and South Poles** – Latitude is measured in terms of the number of degrees north and south from the equator. The North Pole is located at 90°N latitude, while the South Pole is located at 90°S latitude.
- **Tropic of Cancer** – This is the parallel, or latitude, 23½° north of the equator.
- **Tropic of Capricorn** – This is the parallel, or latitude, 23½° south of the equator. The region between these two parallels is the tropics. The subtropics is the area located between 23½° and 40° north and south of the equator.
- **Arctic Circle** – This is the parallel, or latitude, 66½° north of the equator.
- **Antarctic Circle** – This is the parallel, or latitude, 66½° south of the equator.

> **Review Video: Geographical Features**
> Visit mometrix.com/academy and enter code: 773539

78

GPS

Global Positioning System (GPS) is a system of satellites that orbit the Earth and communicate with mobile devices to pinpoint the mobile device's position. This is accomplished by determining the distance between the mobile device and at least three satellites. A mobile device might calculate a distance of 400 miles between it and the first satellite. The possible locations that are 400 miles from the first satellite and the mobile device will fall along a circle. The possible locations on Earth relative to the other two satellites will fall somewhere along different circles. The point on Earth at which these three circles intersect is the location of the mobile device. The process of determining position based on distance measurements from three satellites is called **trilateration**.

> **Review Video: Cartography and Technology**
> Visit mometrix.com/academy and enter code: 642071

Types of Maps

- A **physical map** is one that shows natural features such as mountains, rivers, lakes, deserts, and plains. Color is used to designate the different features.
- A **topographic map** is a type of physical map that shows the relief and configuration of a landscape, such as hills, valleys, fields, forest, roads, and settlements. It includes natural and human-made features.
- A **topological map** is one on which lines are stretched or straightened for the sake of clarity, but retain their essential geometric relationship. This type of map is used, for example, to show the routes of a subway system.
- A **political map** uses lines for state, county, and country boundaries; points or dots for cities and towns; and various other symbols for features such as airports and roads.

Physical and Cultural Features of Geographic Locations and Countries

Physical features:

- **Vegetation zones, or biomes** – Forests, grasslands, deserts, and tundra are the four main types of vegetation zones.
- **Climate zones** – Tropical, dry, temperate, continental, and polar are the five different types of climate zones. Climate is the long-term average weather conditions of a place.

Cultural features:

- **Population density** – This is the number of people living in each square mile or kilometer of a place. It is calculated by dividing population by area.
- **Religion** – This is the identification of the dominant religions of a place, whether Christianity, Hinduism, Judaism, Buddhism, Islam, Shinto, Taoism, or Confucianism. All of these originated in Asia.
- **Languages** – This is the identification of the dominant or official language of a place. There are 12 major language families. The Indo-European family (which includes English, Russian, German, French, and Spanish) is spoken over the widest geographic area, but Mandarin Chinese is spoken by the most people.

> **Review Video: Physical vs. Cultural Geography**
> Visit mometrix.com/academy and enter code: 912136

Coral Reefs

Coral reefs are formed from millions of tiny, tube-shaped **polyps**, an animal life form encased in tough limestone skeletons. Once anchored to a rocky surface, polyps eat plankton and miniscule shellfish caught with poisonous tentacles near the mouth. Polyps use calcium carbonate absorbed from chemicals given off by algae to harden their body armor and cement themselves together in fantastic shapes of many colors. Polyps reproduce through eggs and larvae, but the reef grows by branching out shoots of polyps. There are three types of coral reefs:

- **Fringing reefs** – These surround, or "fringe," an island.
- **Barrier reefs** – Over the centuries, a fringe reef grows so large that the island sinks down from the weight, and the reef becomes a barrier around the island. Water trapped between the island and the reef is called a lagoon.
- **Atolls** – Eventually, the sinking island goes under, leaving the coral reef around the lagoon.

Formation of Mountains

Mountains are formed by the movement of geologic plates, which are rigid slabs of rocks beneath the earth's crust that float on a layer of partially molten rock in the earth's upper mantle. As the plates collide, they push up the crust to form mountains. This process is called **orogeny**. There are three basic forms of orogeny:

- If the collision of continental plates causes the crust to buckle and fold, a chain of **folded mountains**, such as the Appalachians, the Alps, or the Himalayas, is formed.
- If the collision of the plates causes a denser oceanic plate to go under a continental plate, a process called **subduction**; strong horizontal forces lift and fold the margin of the continent. A mountain range like the Andes is the result.
- If an oceanic plate is driven under another oceanic plate, **volcanic mountains** such as those in Japan and the Philippines are formed.

Harmful or Potentially Harmful Interaction with Environment

Wherever humans have gone on the earth, they have made **changes** to their surroundings. Many are harmful or potentially harmful, depending on the extent of the alterations. Some of the changes and activities that can harm the **environment** include:

- Cutting into mountains by machine or blasting to build roads or construction sites
- Cutting down trees and clearing natural growth
- Building houses and cities
- Using grassland to graze herds
- Polluting water sources
- Polluting the ground with chemical and oil waste
- Wearing out fertile land and losing topsoil
- Placing communication lines cross country using poles and wires or underground cable
- Placing railway lines or paved roads cross country
- Building gas and oil pipelines cross country
- Draining wetlands
- Damming up or re-routing waterways
- Spraying fertilizers, pesticides, and defoliants
- Hunting animals to extinction or near extinction

Adaptation to Environmental Conditions

The environment influences the way people live. People **adapt** to **environmental conditions** in ways as simple as putting on warm clothing in a cold environment; finding means to cool their surroundings in an environment with high temperatures; building shelters from wind, rain, and temperature variations; and digging water wells if surface water is unavailable. More complex adaptations result from the physical diversity of the earth in terms of soil, climate, vegetation, and topography. Humans take advantage of opportunities and avoid or minimize limitations. Examples of environmental limitations are that rocky soils offer few opportunities for agriculture and rough terrain limits accessibility. Sometimes, **technology** allows humans to live in areas that were once uninhabitable or undesirable. For example, air conditioning allows people to live comfortably in hot climates; modern heating systems permit habitation in areas with extremely low temperatures, as is the case with research facilities in Antarctica; and airplanes have brought people to previously inaccessible places to establish settlements or industries.

Carrying Capacity and Natural Hazards

Carrying capacity is the maximum, sustained level of use of an environment can incur without sustaining significant environmental deterioration that would eventually lead to environmental destruction. Environments vary in terms of their carrying capacity, a concept humans need to learn to measure and respect before harm is done. Proper **assessment of environmental conditions** enables responsible decision making with respect to how much and in what ways the resources of a particular environment should be consumed. **Energy and water conservation** as well as recycling can extend an area's carrying capacity. In addition to carrying capacity limitations, the physical environment can also have occasional extremes that are costly to humans. **Natural hazards** such as hurricanes, tornadoes, earthquakes, volcanoes, floods, tsunamis, and some forest fires and insect infestations are processes or events that are not caused by humans, but may have serious consequences for humans and the environment. These events are not preventable, and their precise timing, location, and magnitude are not predictable. However, some precautions can be taken to reduce the damage.

Applying Geography to Interpretation of the Past

Space, environment, and chronology are three different points of view that can be used to study history. Events take place within **geographic contexts**. If the world is flat, then transportation choices are vastly different from those that would be made in a round world, for example. Invasions of Russia from the west have normally failed because of the harsh winter conditions, the vast distances that inhibit steady supply lines, and the number of rivers and marshes to be crossed, among other factors. Any invading or defending force anywhere must make choices based on consideration of space and environmental factors. For instance, lands may be too muddy or passages too narrow for certain equipment. Geography played a role in the building of the Panama Canal because the value of a shorter transportation route had to outweigh the costs of labor, disease, political negotiations, and equipment, not to mention a myriad of other effects from cutting a canal through an isthmus and changing a natural land structure as a result.

Applying Geography to Interpretation of the Present and Plans for the Future

The decisions that individual people as well as nations make that may **affect the environment** have to be made with an understanding of spatial patterns and concepts, cultural and transportation connections, physical processes and patterns, ecosystems, and the impact, or "footprint," of people on the physical environment. Sample issues that fit into these considerations are recycling programs, loss of agricultural land to further urban expansion, air and water pollution, deforestation, and ease of transportation and communication. In each of these areas, present and future uses have to be balanced against possible harmful effects. For example, wind is a clean and readily available resource for electric power, but the access roads to and noise of wind turbines can make some areas unsuitable for livestock pasture. Voting citizens need to have an understanding of **geographical and environmental connections** to make responsible decisions.

Spatial Organization

Spatial organization in geography refers to how things or people are grouped in a given space anywhere on earth. Spatial organization applies to the **placement of settlements**, whether hamlets, towns, or cities. These settlements are located to make the distribution of goods and services convenient. For example, in farm communities, people come to town to get groceries, to attend church and school, and to access medical services. It is more practical to provide these things to groups than to individuals. These settlements, historically, have been built close to water sources and agricultural areas. Lands that are topographically difficult, have few resources, or experience extreme temperatures do not have as many people as temperate zones and flat plains, where it is easier to live. Within settlements, a town or city will be organized into commercial and residential neighborhoods, with hospitals, fire stations, and shopping centers centrally located. All of these organizational considerations are spatial in nature.

Themes of Geography

The five themes of geography are:

- **Location** – This includes relative location (described in terms of surrounding geography such as a river, sea coast, or mountain) and absolute location (the specific point of latitude and longitude).
- **Place** – This includes physical characteristics (deserts, plains, mountains, and waterways) and human characteristics (features created by humans, such as architecture, roads, religion, industries, and food and folk practices).
- **Human-environmental interaction** – This includes human adaptation to the environment (using an umbrella when it rains), human modification of the environment (building terraces to prevent soil erosion), and human dependence on the environment for food, water, and natural resources.
- **Movement** –Interaction through trade, migration, communications, political boundaries, ideas, and fashions.
- **Regions** – This includes formal regions (a city, state, country, or other geographical organization as defined by political boundaries), functional regions (defined by a common function or connection, such as a school district), and vernacular regions (informal divisions determined by perceptions or one's mental image, such as the "Far East").

Review Video: Regional Geography
Visit mometrix.com/academy and enter code: 350378

Review Video: Human Geography
Visit mometrix.com/academy and enter code: 195767

82

Geomorphology

The study of landforms is call **geomorphology** or physiography, a science that considers the relationships between *geological structures* and *surface landscape features*. It is also concerned with the processes that change these features, such as erosion, deposition, and plate tectonics. Biological factors can also affect landforms. Examples are when corals build a coral reef or when plants contribute to the development of a salt marsh or a sand dune. Rivers, coastlines, rock types, slope formation, ice, erosion, and weathering are all part of geomorphology. A **landform** is a landscape feature or geomorphological unit. These include hills, plateaus, mountains, deserts, deltas, canyons, mesas, marshes, swamps, and valleys. These units are categorized according to elevation, slope, orientation, stratification, rock exposure, and soil type. Landform elements include pits, peaks, channels, ridges, passes, pools, and plains. The highest order landforms are continents and oceans. Elementary landforms such as segments, facets, and relief units are the smallest homogenous divisions of a land surface at a given scale or resolution.

Oceans, Seas, Lakes, Rivers, and Canals

- **Oceans** are the largest bodies of water on earth and cover nearly 71% of the earth's surface. There are five major oceans: Atlantic, Pacific (largest and deepest), Indian, Arctic, and Southern (surrounds Antarctica).
- **Seas** are smaller than oceans and are somewhat surrounded by land like a lake, but lakes are fresh water and seas are salt water. Seas include the Mediterranean, Baltic, Caspian, Caribbean, and Coral.
- **Lakes** are bodies of water in a depression on the earth's surface. Examples of lakes are the Great Lakes and Lake Victoria.
- **Rivers** are a channeled flow of water that start out as a spring or stream formed by runoff from rain or snow. Rivers flow from higher to lower ground, and usually empty into a sea or ocean. Great rivers of the world include the Amazon, Nile, Rhine, Mississippi, Ganges, Mekong, and Yangtze.
- **Canals** are artificial waterways constructed by humans to connect two larger water bodies. Examples of canals are the Panama and the Suez.

Mountains, Hills, Foothills, Valleys, Plateaus, and Mesas

The definitions for these geographical features are as follows:

- **Mountains** are elevated landforms that rise fairly steeply from the earth's surface to a summit of at least 1,000-2,000 feet (definitions vary) above sea level.
- **Hills** are elevated landforms that rise 500-2,000 feet above sea level.
- **Foothills** are a low series of hills found between a plain and a mountain range.
- **Valleys** are a long depression located between hills or mountains. They are usually products of river erosion. Valleys can vary in terms of width and depth, ranging from a few feet to thousands of feet.
- **Plateaus** are elevated landforms that are fairly flat on top. They may be as high as 10,000 feet above sea level and are usually next to mountains.
- **Mesas** are flat areas of upland. Their name is derived from the Spanish word for table. They are smaller than plateaus and often found in arid or semi-arid areas.

Plains, Deserts, Deltas, and Basins

- **Plains** are extensive areas of low-lying, flat, or gently undulating land, and are usually lower than the landforms around them. Plains near the seacoast are called lowlands.
- **Deserts** are large, dry areas that receive less than 10 inches of rain per year. They are almost barren, containing only a few patches of vegetation.
- **Deltas** are accumulations of silt deposited at river mouths into the seabed. They are eventually converted into very fertile, stable ground by vegetation, becoming important crop-growing areas. Examples include the deltas of the Nile, Ganges, and Mississippi River.
- **Basins** come in various types. They may be low areas that catch water from rivers; large hollows that dip to a central point and are surrounded by higher ground, as in the Donets and Kuznetsk basins in Russia; or areas of inland drainage in a desert when the water can't reach the sea and flows into lakes or evaporates in salt flats as a result. An example is the Great Salt Lake in Utah.

Marshes and Swamps and Tundra and Taiga

Marshes and swamps are both **wet lowlands**. The water can be fresh, brackish, or saline. Both host important ecological systems with unique wildlife. There are, however, some major differences. **Marshes** have no trees and are always wet because of frequent floods and poor drainage that leaves shallow water. Plants are mostly grasses, rushes, reeds, typhas, sedges, and herbs. **Swamps** have trees and dry periods. The water is very slow-moving, and is usually associated with adjacent rivers or lakes.

Both taiga and tundra regions have many plants and animals, but they have few humans or crops because of their harsh climates. **Taiga** has colder winters and hotter summers than tundra because of its distance from the Arctic Ocean. **Tundra** is a Russian word describing marshy plain in an area that has a very cold climate but receives little snow. The ground is usually frozen, but is quite spongy when it is not. Taiga is the world's largest forest region, located just south of the tundra line. It contains huge mineral resources and fur-bearing animals.

Humid Continental, Prairie, Subtropical, and Marine Climates

- A **humid continental climate** is one that has four seasons, including a cold winter and a hot summer, and sufficient rainfall for raising crops. Such climates can be found in the United States, Canada, and Russia. The best farmlands and mining areas are found in these countries.
- **Prairie climates**, or steppe regions, are found in the interiors of Asia and North America where there are dry flatlands (prairies that receive 10-20 inches of rain per year). These dry flatlands can be grasslands or deserts.
- **Subtropical climates** are very humid areas in the tropical areas of Japan, China, Australia, Africa, South America, and the United States. The moisture, carried by winds traveling over warm ocean currents, produces long summers and mild winters. It is possible to produce a continuous cycle of a variety of crops.
- A **marine climate** is one near or surrounded by water. Warm ocean winds bring moisture, mild temperatures year-round, and plentiful rain. These climates are found in Western Europe and parts of the United States, Canada, Chile, New Zealand, and Australia.

Physical and Cultural Geography and Physical and Political Locations

- **Physical geography** is the study of climate, water, and land and their relationships with each other and humans. Physical geography locates and identifies the earth's surface features and explores how humans thrive in various locations according to crop and goods production.
- **Cultural geography** is the study of the influence of the environment on human behaviors as well as the effect of human activities such as farming, building settlements, and grazing livestock on the environment. Cultural geography also identifies and compares the features of different cultures and how they influence interactions with other cultures and the earth.
- **Physical location** refers to the placement of the hemispheres and the continents.
- **Political location** refers to the divisions within continents that designate various countries. These divisions are made with borders, which are set according to boundary lines arrived at by legal agreements.

Both physical and political locations can be precisely determined by geographical surveys and by latitude and longitude.

Natural Resources, Renewable Resources, Nonrenewable Resources, and Commodities

Natural resources are things provided by nature that have commercial value to humans, such as minerals, energy, timber, fish, wildlife, and the landscape. **Renewable resources** are those that can be replenished, such as wind, solar radiation, tides, and water (with proper conservation and clean-up). Soil is renewable with proper conservation and management techniques, and timber can be replenished with replanting. Living resources such as fish and wildlife can replenish themselves if they are not over-harvested. **Nonrenewable resources** are those that cannot be replenished. These include fossil fuels such as oil and coal and metal ores. These cannot be replaced or reused once they have been burned, although some of their products can be recycled. **Commodities** are natural resources that have to be extracted and purified rather than created, such as mineral ores.

Geography

Geography involves learning about the world's primary **physical and cultural patterns** to help understand how the world functions as an interconnected and dynamic system. Combining information from different sources, geography teaches the basic patterns of climate, geology, vegetation, human settlement, migration, and commerce. Thus, geography is an **interdisciplinary** study of history, anthropology, and sociology. **History** incorporates geography in discussions of battle strategies, slavery (trade routes), ecological disasters (the Dust Bowl of the 1930s), and mass migrations. Geographic principles are useful when reading **literature** to help identify and visualize the setting, and also when studying **earth science**, **mathematics** (latitude, longitude, sun angle, and population statistics), and **fine arts** (song, art, and dance often reflect different cultures). Consequently, a good background in geography can help students succeed in other subjects as well.

Areas Covered by Geography

Geography is connected to many issues and provides answers to many everyday questions. Some of the areas covered by geography include:

- Geography investigates global climates, landforms, economies, political systems, human cultures, and migration patterns.
- Geography answers questions not only about where something is located, but also why it is there, how it got there, and how it is related to other things around it.
- Geography explains why people move to certain regions (climate, availability of natural resources, arable land, etc.).
- Geography explains world trade routes and modes of transportation.
- Geography identifies where various animals live and where various crops and forests grow.
- Geography identifies and locates populations that follow certain religions.
- Geography provides statistics on population numbers and growth, which aids in economic and infrastructure planning for cities and countries.

Globe and Map Projections

A **globe** is the only accurate representation of the earth's size, shape, distance, and direction since it, like the earth, is **spherical**. The flat surface of a map distorts these elements. To counter this problem, mapmakers use a variety of "**map projections**," a system for representing the earth's curvatures on a flat surface through the use of a grid that corresponds to lines of latitude and longitude. Some distortions are still inevitable, though, so mapmakers make choices based on the map scale, the size of the area to be mapped, and what they want the map to show. Some projections can represent a true shape or area, while others may be based on the equator and therefore become less accurate as they near the poles. In summary, all maps have some distortion in terms of the shape or size of features of the spherical earth.

Types of Map Projections

There are three main types of map projections:

- **Conical** – This type of projection superimposes a cone over the sphere of the earth, with two reference parallels secant to the globe and intersecting it. There is no distortion along the standard parallels, but distortion increases further from the chosen parallels. A Bonne projection is an example of a conical projection, in which the areas are accurately represented but the meridians are not on a true scale.
- **Cylindrical** – This is any projection in which meridians are mapped using equally spaced vertical lines and circles of latitude (parallels) are mapped using horizontal lines. A Mercator's projection is a modified cylindrical projection that is helpful to navigators because it allows them to maintain a constant compass direction between two points. However, it exaggerates areas in high latitudes.
- **Azimuthal** – This is a stereographic projection onto a plane so centered at any given point that a straight line radiating from the center to any other point represents the shortest distance. This distance can be measured to scale.

Physical Geographical Features to Know to Perform Well in National Geographic Bee

Organizing place names into categories of physical features helps students learn the type of information they need to know to compete in the **National Geographic Bee**. The physical features students need to be knowledgeable about are:

- The continents (Although everyone has been taught that there are seven continents, some geographers combine Europe and Asia into a single continent called Eurasia.)
- The five major oceans
- The highest and lowest points on each continent (Mt. Everest is the highest point in the world; the Dead Sea is the lowest point.)
- The 10 largest seas (The Coral Sea is the largest.)
- The 10 largest lakes (The Caspian Sea is actually the largest lake.)
- The 10 largest islands (Greenland is the largest island.)
- The longest rivers (The Nile is the longest river.)
- Major mountain ranges
- Earth's extremes such as the hottest (Ethiopia), the coldest (Antarctica), the wettest (India), and the driest (Atacama Desert) places; the highest waterfall (Angel Falls); the largest desert (Sahara); the largest canyon (Grand Canyon); the longest reef (Great Barrier Reef); and the highest tides.

Social Studies Skills

Essential Questions Used in Learning Process

Essential questions for learning include those that:

1. Ask for **evaluation, synthesis, and analysis** – the highest levels of Bloom's Taxonomy
2. Seek **information** that is important to know
3. Are worth the student's **awareness**
4. Will result in enduring **understanding**
5. Tend to focus on the questions "**why**?" or "**how** do we know this information?"
6. Are more open-ended and reflective in nature
7. Often address **interrelationships** or lend themselves to multi-disciplinary investigations
8. Spark **curiosity** and a sense of wonder, and invite investigation and activity
9. Can be asked **over and over** and in a variety of instances
10. Encourage related questions
11. Have answers that may be **extended** over time
12. Seek to identify key understandings
13. Engage students in **real-life**, applied problem solving
14. May not be answerable without a **lifetime of investigation**, and maybe not even then

Various Disciplines of Social Studies

- **Anthropology and sociology** provide an understanding of how the world's many cultures have developed and what these cultures and their values have to contribute to society.
- **Sociology, economics, and political science** provide an understanding of the institutions in society and each person's role within social groups. These topics teach the use of charts, graphs, and statistics.

- **Political science, civics, and government** teach how to see another person's point of view, accept responsibility, and deal with conflict. They also provide students with an understanding of democratic norms and values, such as justice and equality. Students learn how to apply these norms and values in their community, school, and family.
- **Economics** teaches concepts such as work, exchange (buying, selling, and other trade transactions), production of goods and services, the origins of materials and products, and consumption.
- **Geography** teaches students how to use maps, globes, and locational and directional terms. It also provides them with an understanding of spatial environments, landforms, climate, world trade and transportation, ecological systems, and world cultures.

Constructivist Learning Theory and Information Seeking Behavior Theory

The **Constructivist Learning Theory** supports a view of inquiry-based learning as an opportunity for students to experience learning through inquiry and problem solving. This process is characterized by exploration and risk taking, curiosity and motivation, engagement in critical and creative thinking, and connections with real-life situations and real audiences. The **Information Seeking Behavior Theory** purports that students progress through levels of question specificity, from vague notions of the information needed to clearly defined needs or questions. According to this theory, students are more successful in the search process if they have a realistic understanding of the information system and problem. They should understand that the inquiry process is not linear or confined to certain steps, but is a flexible, individual process that leads back to the original question.

Study of Cultures and Community Relations

An important part of social studies, whether anthropology, sociology, history, geography, or political science, is the study of **local and world cultures**, as well as individual community dynamics. Students should be able to:

- Identify **values** held by their own culture and community
- Identify **values** held by other cultures and communities
- Recognize the **influences** of other cultures on their own culture
- Identify major **social institutions** and their roles in the students' communities
- Understand how individuals and groups **interact** to obtain food, clothing, and shelter
- Understand the role of language, literature, the arts, and traditions in a culture
- Recognize the role of **media and technology** in cultures, particularly in the students' own cultures
- Recognize the influence of various types of **government, economics, the environment, and technology** on social systems and cultures
- Evaluate the effectiveness of **social institutions** in solving problems in a community or culture
- Examine changes in **population, climate, and production**, and evaluate their effects on the community or culture

Types of Maps and Scale

There are three basic types of maps:

- **Base maps** – Created from aerial and field surveys, base maps serve as the starting point for topographic and thematic maps.
- **Topographic maps** – These show the natural and human-made surface features of the earth, including mountain elevations, river courses, roads, names of lakes and towns, and county and state lines.
- **Thematic maps** – These use a base or topographic map as the foundation for showing data based on a theme, such as population density, wildlife distribution, hill-slope stability, economic trends, etc.

Scale is the size of a map expressed as a ratio of the actual size of the land (for example, 1 inch on a map represents 1 mile on land). In other words, it is the proportion between a distance on the map and its corresponding distance on earth. The scale determines the level of detail on a map. **Small-scale maps** depict larger areas, but include fewer details. **Large-scale maps** depict smaller areas, but include more details.

Time Zones

Time is linked to **longitude** in that a complete rotation of the Earth, or 360° of longitude, occurs every 24 hours. Each hour of time is therefore equivalent to 15° of longitude, or 4 minutes for each 1° turn. By the agreement of 27 nations at the 1884 International Meridian Conference, the time zone system consists of **24 time zones** corresponding to the 24 hours in a day. Although high noon technically occurs when the sun is directly above a meridian, calculating time that way would result in 360 different times for the 360 meridians. Using the 24-hour system, the time is the same for all locations in a 15° zone. The 1884 conference established the meridian passing through Greenwich, England, as the zero point, or **prime meridian**. The halfway point is found at the 180th meridian, a half day from Greenwich. It is called the **International Date Line**, and serves as the place where each day begins and ends on earth.

Cartography

Cartography is the art and science of **mapmaking**. Maps of local areas were drawn by the Egyptians as early as 1300 BC, and the Greeks began making maps of the known world in the 6th century BC. Cartography eventually grew into the field of geography. The first step in modern mapmaking is a **survey**. This involves designating a few key sites of known elevation as benchmarks to allow for measurement of other sites. **Aerial photography** is then used to chart the area by taking photos in sequence. Overlapping photos show the same area from different positions along the flight line. When paired and examined through a stereoscope, the cartographer gets a three-dimensional view that can be made into a **topographical map**. In addition, a field survey (on the ground) is made to determine municipal borders and place names. The second step is to compile the information and **computer-draft** a map based on the collected data. The map is then reproduced or printed.

Skills and Materials Needed to Be Successful in Social Studies Course

For classes in history, geography, civics/government, anthropology, sociology, and economics, the goal is for students to explore issues and learn key concepts. **Social studies** help improve communication skills in reading and writing, but students need sufficient **literacy skills** to be able to understand specialized vocabulary, identify key points in text, differentiate between fact and

89

opinion, relate information across texts, connect prior knowledge and new information, and synthesize information into meaningful knowledge. These literacy skills will be enhanced in the process, and will extend into higher order thinking skills that enable students to compare and contrast, hypothesize, draw inferences, explain, analyze, predict, construct, and interpret. Social studies classes also depend on a number of different types of **materials beyond the textbook**, such as nonfiction books, biographies, journals, maps, newspapers (paper or online), photographs, and primary documents.

Benefits of Social Studies for Students

Social studies cover the political, economic, cultural, and environmental aspects of societies not only in the past, as in the study of history, but also in the present and future. Students gain an understanding of **current conditions** and learn how to prepare for the **future** and cope with **change** through studying geography, economics, anthropology, government, and sociology. Social studies classes teach assessment, problem solving, evaluation, and decision making skills in the context of good citizenship. Students learn about scope and sequence, designing investigations, and following up with research to collect, organize, and present information and data. In the process, students learn how to search for patterns and their meanings in society and in their own lives. Social studies build a **positive self-concept** within the context of understanding the similarities and differences of people. Students begin to understand that they are unique, but also share many feelings and concerns with others. As students learn that each individual can contribute to society, their self-awareness builds self-esteem.

Inquiry-Based Learning

Facilitated by the teacher who models, guides, and poses a starter question, **inquiry-based learning** is a process in which students are involved in their learning. This process involves formulating questions, investigating widely, and building new understanding and meaning. This combination of steps asks students to think independently, and enables them to answer their questions with new knowledge, develop solutions, or support a position or point of view. In inquiry-based learning activities, teachers engage students, ask for authentic assessments, require research using a variety of resources (books, interviews, Internet information, etc.), and involve students in cooperative interaction. All of these require the **application of processes and skills**. Consequently, new knowledge is usually shared with others, and may result in some type of action. Inquiry-based learning focuses on finding a solution to a question or a problem, whether it is a matter of curiosity, a puzzle, a challenge, or a disturbing confusion.

Credibility of Research Sources

Some sources are not reliable, so the student must have a means to evaluate the **credibility** of a source when doing research, particularly on the Internet. The value of a source depends on its intended use and whether it fits the subject. For example, students researching election campaigns in the 19th century would need to go to historical documents, but students researching current election practices could use candidate brochures, television advertisements, and web sites. A checklist for examining sources might include:

- Check the **authority and reputation** of the author, sponsoring group, or publication
- Examine the language and illustrations for **bias**
- Look for a clear, logical **arrangement** of information
- If online, check out the associated links, archives, contact ability, and the date of last update

Common Research Methods in Social Sciences

Social science research relies heavily on **empirical research**, which is original data gathering and analysis through direct observation or experiment. It also involves using the library and Internet to obtain raw data, locate information, or review expert opinion. Because social science projects are often interdisciplinary, students may need assistance from the librarian to find related search terms. While arguments still exist about the superiority of quantitative versus qualitative research, most social scientists understand that research is an eclectic mix of the two methods. **Quantitative research** involves using techniques to gather data, which is information dealing with numbers and measurable values. Statistics, tables, and graphs are often the products. **Qualitative research** involves non-measurable factors, and looks for meaning in the numbers produced by quantitative research. Qualitative research takes data from observations and analyzes it to find underlying meanings and patterns of relationships.

WEST-E ELA Practice Test

1. Which of the following students may need extra instruction and evaluation with respect to oral language skills?

    a. Rosa: whose first language is Spanish. Rosa speaks with a distinct accent and can be difficult to understand when speaking about a new or unfamiliar topic.

    b. Greer: who avoids oral assignments when possible. He avoids speaking up in class and only responds when called upon.

    c. Ashley: who often has trouble answering questions in class. Her responses are often off-topic. She also struggles with oral presentations, seeming to present a string of unrelated facts.

    d. Brett: who frequently becomes loud and disruptive whenever group work is assigned. He often becomes involved in heated discussions with classmates when discussing ideas.

2. Mr. Callas is introducing a unit on oral traditions from around the world. He wants his seventh-grade students to gain a better understanding of the relationship between written text and oral language, as well as increase their multi-cultural understanding. Which of the following assignments would be the most relevant?

    a. "Read Chapter 12 on Oral Traditions and complete the end-of-chapter review."

    b. "Select a poem or song from a culture around the world and recite it for the class."

    c. "Conduct a poll of twenty fellow students, asking about their family's country of origin. Present a graph or diagram of your results in class."

    d. "Choose a country to research and write a first-person narrative about a typical day in the life of one of its citizens. The narratives will be read in class."

3. Which of the following exercises would be the most appropriate tool for helping students evaluate the effectiveness of their own spoken messages?

    a. Discuss written and oral assignments in class before completing them. Once the assignments are completed, the teacher meets individually with each student to discuss the content and effectiveness of each student's work.

    b. Instruct students to present oral reports in class, which are then "graded" by classmates. A score of 1-10 is assigned based on students' perception of the reports' clarity. The student's average score determines his report's effectiveness.

    c. Ask each student to prepare an oral report and a content quiz that highlights the report's main idea. The student then uses classmates' scores on the reviews to determine his report's effectiveness.

    d. Put students into groups of three. Two students complete a role-playing assignment based on prompts provided by the teacher. The third student gives constructive feedback on how the other two can refine and clarify their speech.

Use the following information to answer the next two questions.

Mr. Gilbert teaches fourth graders whose reading skills range from emergent to advanced. He introduces an activity called "Book Buddies" in which his students are paired with emerging Kindergarten readers to practice reading beginner-level short books. He hopes they will gain confidence and increase their own reading skills through these visits. Mr. Gilbert's students pick their Book Buddies up once a week and read together for about half an hour.

4. What aspect of this program is most likely to increase all of the fourth-graders' oral language skills?

a. Finding opportunities to explain unfamiliar ideas or sound out new words with the younger students.
b. Spending time with younger students and being reminded of how much they have learned in the past three years.
c. Being exposed to different kinds of reading texts.
d. Practicing their decoding skills and increasing their vocabulary.

5. What might be the best way to adapt the Book Buddy program for fourth grade students who are still learning English?

a. Exempt ESOL students from the program altogether so that they can practice reading with their primary teacher.
b. Create some groups that have three Book Buddies: a skilled reader, an ESOL student, and a Kindergartener; this will allow the English language learner to listen, learn, and give guidance when he is able.
c. Make no changes to the program and simply allow the younger students and the English language learner to help each other decode and compare ideas in their own way.
d. Allow English language learners to listen to books on tape read by native English speakers with their Kindergarten partners.

6. Mr. Campbell begins each Language Arts lesson with the "Phrase of the Day." This phrase ranges from analogies to idioms to snippets of figurative language. His students use their journals to explain what they think the phrase means and to draw a picture, also. Mr. Campbell then reveals the phrase's true meaning, which the children record on the same page as their own interpretations. When he reviews these pages in the students' journals, Mr. Campbell is most likely to:

a. Check to ensure that each student is diligently recording both their own interpretations and the correct interpretations.
b. Use the mechanics and spelling errors within to help him design test questions and worksheets.
c. Grade the pages for originality and humor.
d. Use them to informally assess students' oral language skills.

7. Which of the following activities would incorporate the best use of technology to increase students' oral language skills?

    a. Students visit the school computer lab to work on math and science activities with software that utilizes voice-recognition technology in an interactive process.

    b. Students use an internet program and computer camera to converse with English-speaking students in other countries.

    c. Students can visit the classroom's Language Lab, in which there are tape recorders and CD players. Students can use these players to listen to novels, poetry, and other literary works on tape.

    d. A teacher videotapes a class discussion about a story and replays it for the students to watch and discuss.

8. Every year, students prepare with excitement for Historical Characters Day. Each student is expected to choose a character who was influential in years past and compose a report on why he was important. The students are permitted to dress up as their respective characters on the day on which the reports are turned in. This year, the teachers want to incorporate an aspect of this anticipated event that will more directly increase their students' oral communication skills. Of the options they have brainstormed, which of the following would be most helpful?

    a. Ask the students to read their reports aloud to the class.

    b. Require that the reports be memorized so that students can make better use of voice modulation and eye contact while presenting.

    c. Require the students to write why they chose their character and three interesting things they learned on a set note cards, and present what they have written to the class.

    d. Hold an election for the student with the most realistic costume and require students to give supporting evidence for their votes.

Use the information below to answer the questions 9 and 10:

A middle school teacher consistently includes "the Daily Chat" in her lesson plans, several times a week. Students are placed into pairs, with the occasional group of three. The teacher chooses one student during each chat with whom she will partner. During these conversations, students can pick a topic and discuss it for five to ten minutes. They are asked to use the following log sheet:

Date:

Name:

Partner's Name:

☐ My partner looked at me most of the time while we were speaking.

☐ My partner listened while I was speaking.

☐ My partner waited until I finished before taking his turn to speak.

☐ My partner enunciated while speaking (I understood the words he was saying).

☐ My partner explained himself well (I understood the ideas behind what he was saying).

9. Which skill is least likely to be improved by this activity?
   a. Active listening; students listen for the purpose of understanding and responding appropriately.
   b. Speaking clearly; students practice speaking in ways that can be easily heard and understood.
   c. Nonverbal communication skills; students communicate engagement in conversation through body language, etc.
   d. Oral conflict resolution; students can resolve disagreements using their verbal skills.

10. What is the most likely purpose for the teacher to partner with a new student during each Daily Chat?
   a. She wants to make sure that the students get positive feedback on a regular basis during skill-building exercises.
   b. She has found that there are almost always absent students, creating a space for her to function as a partner during days where one student lacks a partner.
   c. She recognizes the value of building oral communication skills with adults as well as peers.
   d. She wants to demonstrate how to resolve conflicts or common problems that students often face when attempting to communicate effectively.

11. The eighth-grade class will be holding class elections in the fall as part of an integrated Social Studies and English unit. The students will be studying government elections and modeling their process based on their studies. The candidates for Vice President and President will debate pre-determined issues in front of their class using modified rules found in formal debates (i.e. they are timed and will use a moderator). Which of the following exercises would be most beneficial to introduce in English class to help prepare each student for the debates?

a. Watch recordings of Presidential and Vice Presidential debates from years past and model their speech from what they have heard.

b. Create multiple opportunities for students to discuss the pre-determined issues in class, allowing for free-flowing dialogue and differing opinions.

c. Students write their thoughts in short-essay format so that each section can be read aloud during the appropriate part of the debate.

d. Students determine a position on each selected issue and assign it to a note card or small piece of paper. On each card, they record two to three reasons or supporting ideas for the opinion.

12. A teacher wants to work on her students' listening comprehension in addition to their reading comprehension, since she understands that the skills are interrelated. She has a series of short stories that she thinks the students will enjoy. Which of the following would be the best supplement to typical written comprehension exercises?

a. Preview content and then read the stories aloud to the students. Assess listening comprehension through verbal and written questions.

b. Ask the students to choose one story each to read aloud to a small group. Encourage the students to discuss what they have learned afterward.

c. Assign each student a story to read and require them to write a report on it. Each student should then present his report based on what he has learned to the class.

d. Have the students read stories aloud to the class, and create mock tests based upon the main ideas which they identify.

13. Ms. Walters wants to help her brand-new group of still-emergent fourth-grade students build comprehension skills. Which of the following exercises would be the best way to quickly gauge the students' current comprehension levels during the first week of class?

a. Provide the students with instruction-level text to be read independently. Hold an in-class discussion about what happened in the story.

b. Read a story aloud to the class and then ask each student to draw three pictures representing the beginning, middle and end of the story.

c. Put students into group or pairs to read the story aloud. Each group then collaborates to answer the story review questions.

d. Have each student re-tell the story to the class in his own words.

14. Which of the following strategies would not be helpful in building the word-identification skills of emergent readers?

a. Allowing for invented spelling in written assignments or in class work.

b. Reinforcing phonemic awareness while reading aloud.

c. Using dictionaries to look up unfamiliar words.

d. Studying and reviewing commonly-used sight words at the students' ability level.

15. Mrs. Harris is pleased that her fifth-graders are showing progress in their reading comprehension and writing skills. The students are performing very well on their written tests, evaluations, and homework. After the holiday break, she wants to design lessons that increase the students' literacy skills by incorporating multiple contexts. Which of the following might be the best way to do this?

a. Read their next book aloud and discuss it in class.
b. Have the students quiz one another in small groups on the content of their textbooks and other reading assignments.
c. Read a play in class and allow the students to act it out for their peers following their unit test.
d. Administer spelling and vocabulary tests orally to determine students' verbal skills.

16. Which of the following would be most useful in assessing and documenting students' language progress throughout a school year?

a. An audio/video recording of each student reading the same text at the beginning of the year and again at the end of the year
b. A portfolio including pre-tests, post-tests, vocabulary work, journal entries, writing assignments, group projects and other relevant work from throughout the year
c. Score composites and details from state- and national-referenced exams or other standardized tests.
d. A detailed narrative composed by the student's teacher, detailing strengths, weaknesses, and descriptions of the student's work.

17. Valeria is a bright sixth-grader who struggles with reading fluency. She comes from a predominantly Spanish-speaking home and has only lived in the United States for two years. Her teacher plans to use the guided oral reading strategy to help increase Valeria's reading skills. Which of the following would not be a part of this strategy?

a. Valeria is partnered with another student who is also struggling with language fluency in class.
b. Valeria's partner reads a given text aloud and then gives her a chance to read the text silently several times.
c. Valeria reads the text aloud three to four times.
d. Valeria's partner gives encouragement and feedback.

18. Mr. Waleran requires his students of all ability levels to write freely in their journals twice a week. While students are encouraged to use proper spelling and mechanics as much as possible, the purpose behind this activity is to encourage students to express themselves through writing without concern for grading parameters. How should he adapt this activity for Dimitri, who has several academic delays that keep him from reading and writing in legible or coherent ways?

a. Allow Dimitri to dictate his thoughts to another student or teacher who will then record them into his journal in writing.
b. Encourage Dimitri to draw pictures in his journal that represent his thoughts, and encourage him to use the words he knows to label or describe the pictures.
c. Tell Dimitri to keep an audio journal at home, using a personal tape recorder.
d. Require Dimitri to attempt to write in complete sentences as much as he can, and then edit the journal together for spelling and mechanical errors.

19. A teacher reads to her students at least once a week. This month, she plans to read poetry to her class. The students will then discuss what they have heard for the rest of each class period. What is this teacher's most likely purpose in designing these lessons?

    a. To give students a break from extensive reading requirements.
    b. To build phonological awareness, specifically of rhyming words.
    c. To teach students that there is more to literature than prose.
    d. To increase students' listening skills while exposing them to new kinds of literature.

20. Mrs. Taylor is working with a diverse group of fifth-graders. She introduces a lesson and project that students can work on once they have finished their regular class work. Students may visit a section of the classroom where they can listen to a lesson via headphones on ancient Egyptian hieroglyphics and look at various library books on the subject. Students are then expected to create their own hieroglyphics that they can use to tell a short story. Which of the following skills is not built with this project?

    a. Understanding of various kinds of written expression, including non-alphabetic languages.
    b. Building multi-cultural awareness that will increase understanding between students of different backgrounds.
    c. Reading for purposes of information or new knowledge (i.e. 'reading to learn').
    d. Exposure to various media to build literacy skills across all levels of reading ability.

21. Each week, a teacher asks one student to bring in a recording of his favorite song and a written version of the lyrics. The students listen to the song and receive a copy of the lyrics. They discuss these words as either one large group or in small groups. What are these students probably learning from this exercise?

    a. Students are learning about the lives of their peers indirectly by listening to each student's favorite song; they can begin to understand each other by the meaning behind the song lyrics.
    b. Students are learning that they are very diverse in many ways: they have different musical tastes and prefer many different styles of music and expression.
    c. Students are learning that it is very difficult to communicate freely when bound by various musical traits such as rhyming, rhythm, and phrasing.
    d. Students are learning that literacy skills do not just pertain to schoolwork. These skills allow students to understand and communicate meanings through a variety of ways, including music and lyrics.

22. A teacher notices that one of her students is inconsistent with recalling his letter-sounds. He may remember a particular sound or blend one day and read it correctly; however, the next day, he may not be able to produce the same sound. What should she do?

    a. Immediately refer the student to the appropriate professional for educational testing since it is likely that he is exhibiting early signs of a learning difference or disability.
    b. Recognize that children all learn at different rates and that learning and producing letter-sounds involve multiple mental processes. Give the student as much time as he needs to internalize the sounds and produce them correctly.
    c. Provide the student with targeted instruction in letter-sound correspondence, using a schema such as Alphabet Action, in which letter-sounds are associated with physical actions (e.g., C is for Catch). Set a time frame after which, if the student does not improve, to begin the procedure for special-needs testing.
    d. Hold a conference with the child's parents and encourage them to seek outside tutoring or professional assistance with his reading skills.

23. Mrs. Bundy has three groups of students in her fifth-grade English class: those who want to answer every question, those who only speak when spoken to, and those who never speak at all. She is making plans for upcoming lessons and thinks about the last group of children who never speak up in class. What is important for Mrs. Bundy to know and do with respect to these students?

a. Know that some students are simply quiet and do not feel comfortable speaking up in class. As long as the children are completing their work accurately, do not be concerned about them.
b. Speak with those students after or before class. Let them know how important it is to express themselves in class, because that is part of what building literacy is all about.
c. Make a point to speak directly to those students who talk less in class. Limit the amount of time the more verbal students can speak in class and require the quieter students to answer more direct questions and prompts.
d. Place students who don't speak up in class together for group work. Make a point to spend time with those groups to give guidance and encouragement as they express their ideas verbally.

24. Some of the students in Mr. Smith's fourth-grade class cannot decode words well enough to read fluently in class. He knows they are well behind grade level and that he needs to provide them with activities that will allow them to be successful, building skills and confidence at the same time. Which activity would be best for this purpose?

a. Enlist the parents' help by sending home a weekly list of sight words that the students can practice and memorize, decreasing the need to decode when they read.
b. Show the students how to create words out of movable alphabet tiles or magnetic letters, building (encoding) words as they sound them out.
c. Provide the children with early childhood readers that contain only very simple words so that the children will not feel badly as they read.
d. Allow those children having trouble to stop each time they reach a challenging word and sound it out carefully, recording it to a list that will be studied for homework.

25. Which of the following statements is true regarding the relationship of reading fluency to reading comprehension?

a. Reading fluency and reading comprehension should be considered separate, equally valuable skills that can be taught independently of one another.
b. Reading comprehension is an important component of achieving a level of overall reading fluency.
c. Reading fluency refers to a set of skills that should be continually improved upon, so that students can consistently comprehend that which they read.
d. Reading comprehension and reading fluency are so intertwined that a child struggling in one area is often incapable of making progress in the other.

26. Abi, a fifth-grader, is reading aloud to his teacher during one-on-one reading time. His teacher uses this time to evaluate ongoing fluency and comprehension skills. Following today's reading, Abi's teacher determines that he needs practice with words that begin with digraphs. Which of the following sets of words would most likely be part of this assignment?

a. Chicken, Shells, That
b. Were, Frame, Click
c. Sponge, Think, Blank
d. Packed, Blistered, Smoothed

27. Which of the following generally would not be expected of an eighth-grader?

a. Identify grade-level vocabulary words and be able to decode their roots, prefixes, and suffixes, as well as non-English words that are commonly used in English writing (e.g. phenomenon, charisma, etc.).
b. Analyze literary works and identify common themes in various pieces of literature.
c. Understand different points of view in literature (e.g. omniscient, subjective)
d. Explain how media messages are reflective of the literature in cultures from which they originate.

28. Which of the following reading skills might be most helpful for Susannah?

Susannah wrote the following journal entry on her happiest memory during journal time:
I lov going on picnics with my mom and dad. We et sandwitches and lemanad and somtyms mom and dad drink coffee. we play gams and haf fun.

a. Decoding work focusing on silent ending phonemes.
b. Sight word drills and practice.
c. Reading aloud to a partner who gives constructive feedback.
d. More spelling practice using original sentences.

29. A teacher writes four sentences on the board and instructs his students to copy the sentences from the board into their notebooks. They must capitalize words with suffixes. Which sentence is correct?

a. The PRINCE declared his undying love for the PRINCESS.
b. Television is a form of MULTIMEDIA.
c. This loud, loud noise is very DISPLEASING.
d. The BOOKKEEPER examined every page of the rare play.

30. Which of the following computer activities/games would be most beneficial during media time for students who are working on reading fluency?

a. Students can select from a variety of high-interest texts and read aloud what they see on the screen.
b. Students hear high-frequency sight and vocabulary words in their headphones and get points for "zapping" (clicking) the correct matching word on their screen.
c. Students practice typing in a keyboarding program to build their speed and accuracy in writing reports and papers.
d. Students can surf a limited and pre-approved number of internet sites to read on subjects of their choosing.

31. A teacher is fortunate to have many parent volunteers for the current school year, giving him parental help at least three times a week. He wants to utilize these volunteers in a way that will not only take into account their limited training, but will most benefit students. Which option should he choose?

a. Ask each parent to speak to the class about what kinds of literacy skills they use each day in their careers.
b. Enlist parents to help grade papers and presentations using a rubric.
c. Ask parents to listen to his students read challenging but manageable texts, one at a time, helping students identify and sound out unfamiliar words.
d. Primarily utilize parents' for non-instructional tasks, such as making copies, organizing the class library, monitoring the classroom during test time, etc.

32. Which of the following aspects of oral reading is the most important accompaniment to speed and accuracy?

   a. Vocal expression based on punctuation and content.
   b. Volume of the reader's/speaker's voice.
   c. Interest level of the text to be read aloud.
   d. Consistently increasing the number of words read aloud per minute.

33. Which of the following activities is widely used in building students' reading fluency?

   a. Sole focus on phonetic instruction.
   b. Repeated oral readings combined with feedback.
   c. Participation in vocabulary-building activities.
   d. Utilizing speed-reading techniques often used in adult literacy courses.

34. In monitoring a group of elementary-age students' reading fluency, which of the following students may need extra or specialized instruction?

   a. A student who reads an unfamiliar text more slowly than he reads a familiar text.
   b. A student reading an independent-level text, finding approximately 1 in 25 words difficult to read.
   c. A student reading an instructional-level text, finding approximately 1 in 5 words difficult to read.
   d. A student who scores a 70% on a comprehension test.

35. Which of the following reading assignments would be most appropriate as a context for teaching students how to preview information to improve comprehension?

   a. A written version of a popular movie that most of the students have seen outside of class.
   b. A reading assignment from the students' science class that they will be tested on next month.
   c. A novel the students read in English class last year.
   d. A set of poems that will be studied next month during Poetry Week.

36. A sixth-grade teacher is preparing to begin a unit in which students will be reading a novel in class. She plans to use the novel to teach her students specific strategies to improve and monitor their reading comprehension. Which of the following techniques would likely be taught during class?

   a. Discuss story elements such as exposition, climax and resolution.
   b. Demonstrate the practice of stopping at the end of chapters to summarize and review the content.
   c. Ask students to complete a review sheet before taking the unit test.
   d. Practice decoding unfamiliar words throughout the book by using knowledge of frequently-used root words.

37. A teacher notices that her new student, Carl, has a hard time answering questions related to comprehension during class and has scored low on comprehension quizzes and worksheets. What would be the most logical first step in determining how to help Carl?

    a. Encourage Carl to read all assigned texts at least twice before class to help him understand what he has read.

    b. Provide Carl with story maps of what he will be reading to assist his comprehension visually.

    c. Ask Carl to read aloud with his teacher individually so that she can ensure that he is reading with expected accuracy and speed (i.e., fluently).

    d. Modify Carl's class work so that he is able to work on easier comprehension material until his skills are brought up to speed.

38. Which of the following would be the best strategy for helping eighth-grade students choose books that they will read independently and use to write book reports?

    a. Provide two choices from which the students can pick that you know everybody can understand.

    b. Allow students to freely pick their books, but require that they read a few pages aloud to you in order to ensure that the reading level is neither too easy nor too difficult based on their abilities.

    c. Encourage the students to read a book that contains unfamiliar words and idioms so that they will be challenged to use context clues, dictionaries and other sources to build comprehension.

    d. Establish no parameters on book selection to encourage free choice and promote students' excitement about the project.

39. Which of the following students is not performing "at grade level" and may warrant academic support or testing?

    a. Karishma, seventh grade, looks panicked and becomes very quiet when asked to state her opinion about a particular subject in class discussions and rarely raises her hand when a question about text comprehension is posed.

    b. Lynne, fifth grade, is able to comprehend most of what she reads in plays and in fiction, but sometimes has trouble understanding poetry.

    c. Barron, sixth grade, can read fluently aloud and often recall concrete facts, but is rarely able to draw conclusions, make inferences, or understand figurative language.

    d. Sebastien, eighth grade, lacks motivation to read much of what is assigned in class and frequently fails to complete his homework; he often contributes intelligently to class discussions.

Use the following information to answer questions 40 and 41:

> Autumn must be the most enchanting season of all. The wind takes on a _____ chill that, when inhaled, _____ with the scent of ____ wood to lightly and_____singe your throat! Statuesque ____ seem to erupt into ____ blooms of colors seen ____ no other time, except _____ inside boxes of children's ____. For many people, the ____of camping, cookouts, sports, ____school creates warm, tingling ____ of security as the _____ slowly turns from Summer _____Fall. There is no other day in the year like the first day of Autumn.

40. The passage above is an example of what kind of reading comprehension assessment?
    a. Vocabulary Memorization Test
    b. Cloze Individual Assessment
    c. Student Response Form
    d. Figurative Language Assessment

41. In determining his students' reading comprehension levels, a teacher uses the above passage. He finds that about half of Anne's answers make sense in the blanks. Which answer choice describes the level at which Anne is reading the text?
    a. instructional level
    b. independent level
    c. frustration level
    d. novice level

42. Which of the following practices would assist students in constructing meaning from a fictional text written long before the students were born?
    a. After the text is read for homework, students discuss any aspects of the story that they did not understand or that were unfamiliar to them.
    b. Students individually visualize scenery and events in the text as they read.
    c. The class makes a list of unfamiliar words in the text and looks them up in the dictionary as the text is read.
    d. Before the text is assigned, students learn about pertinent historical events or aspects of culture that informed the writing of the text.

43. Which of the following strategies would be most appropriate for increasing comprehension before reading a chapter book without pictures?
    a. Previewing the chapter titles and identifying questions that would be answered by reading.
    b. Predicting the ending of the story after reading the introduction and first chapter of the book.
    c. Discussing what the students have heard from other individuals about the story.
    d. Researching and reading book reviews to get an idea of what experts have said about the story.

44. Which of these sets of factors would most greatly affect a student's reading comprehension in class and on tests?
    a. Oral language development, written language development and eating a healthy breakfast.
    b. Word analysis skills, sight word knowledge and ability to monitor understanding.
    c. Vocabulary development, sight word knowledge and reference skills.
    d. Prior knowledge, good classroom participation and academic performance in other subjects.

45. A teacher assigns a project in which students must compare excerpts from the Charles Dickens novel they are reading in class and an article from the week's newspaper. The teacher has chosen a specific passage from the novel. The students can choose the newspaper excerpts, as long as they are of similar lengths. The students must then write a short essay comparing the two. What is this teacher hoping to show her students?

a. That Dickens' writing style is journalistic and that he informed much of what is considered to be current journalistic philosophy.
b. That there are links between the students' lives and what they read in class; the relationships are there if they make an effort to see them.
c. That you can compare even two unlike things.
d. That there are distinct differences between the way meaning is constructed in daily life and in literature; different processes must be applied.

46. A seventh-grade teacher wants to encourage her students to read more for pleasure. She knows that the students' comprehension, vocabulary and writing skills will also be improved by reading more frequently. What is the best way to increase the amount of time students spend reading for pleasure?

a. Assign "extra-credit" in which students can write a book report on a favorite book they read as a child.
b. Increase the number of books and poems included in each unit of study.
c. Ask the students to read a text of their choosing (e.g., a magazine, comic book, internet source, novel) each week and present to the class what they enjoyed about it.
d. Have each student make a list of books they would like to read someday and then create a timeline for when they want to complete each one.

47. Students in Mr. Carmen's class receive a list of words each month that make up their spelling and vocabulary work. They are expected to write the words in original sentences to help them remember spellings and meanings of each one. Mr. Carmen also, however, wants to build the students' vocabulary using indirect learning styles. Which of the following would not contribute to learning vocabulary indirectly?

a. Assigning more complex "bonus words" each month that can be written and defined for extra credit.
b. Expecting students to read a weekly newspaper.
c. Watching an instructional-level video in class and discussing any unknown words.
d. Asking students to complete a series of short interviews with adults in their lives.

48. Which of the following vocabulary activities would best prepare students for a unit on imagery and figurative language?

a. A class discussion on the difference between literal and inferential comprehension.
b. A worksheet on synonyms and antonyms.
c. A set of word games (e.g., crosswords, word searches) involving adjectives and adverbs.
d. A vocabulary quiz

Use the following information to answer questions 49 and 50:

A class considers the paragraph below:

Sarah and Kelly grinned at one another conspiratorially as they approached Dad, who was quietly reading his paper in the living room. "Dad, we'd like to ride our bikes down to Emil's house today," giggled Kelly. She glanced at her sister and shifted her weight from foot to foot. Dad appeared to think this over for a moment and replied, "Sure, that's fine with me!" The girls scampered to get their bikes and were soon on their way. With the children gone, Dad noticed how peaceful and quiet the house sounded. His reverie was quickly interrupted as he heard Mom calling from upstairs, "okay, everybody, I told you at breakfast that I need as much help as I can get to help me give the dog a bath, clean the house and finish the laundry today!" Dad groaned, knowing that he had been conned!

49. Which method would be best for helping students determine the meaning of the word "reverie" in the next to last sentence?
   a. Using context clues
   b. Making an educated guess
   c. Decoding the prefix, root, and suffix of the word
   d. Previewing and reviewing

50. Which of the following questions, when assigned as an in-class writing topic, would allow the teacher to monitor the children's inferential comprehension?
   a. What do you think the girls plan to do at Emil's once they arrive?
   b. What does it mean to say that Dad had been "conned?"
   c. Why is it important for everyone to help Mom with the chores?
   d. What did Dad enjoy so much while he was reading?

51. Which of the following choices shows the correct type of text matched with an appropriate strategy for increasing reading comprehension?
   a. Popular magazine: critical analysis/deconstruction
   b. Literary novel: key concept synthesis
   c. Persuasive essay: journaling over time, recording personal thoughts about the reading
   d. Chapter from science textbook: text outlining with vocabulary and main ideas

52. Students in an eighth grade class examine this vocabulary list on Monday. Which literary genre is likely to be introduced this week?

> Vocabulary:
> Narrative
> Heroism
> Ancient
> Martyr
> Duality
> Supernatural
> Deity
> Culture

    a. Historical Fiction
    b. Poetry
    c. Mythology
    d. Drama

53. Which question below applies most closely to data analysis skills for Mrs. Layton's fifth-graders?

Our Hobbies	
Reading	8
Soccer	4
Dance	3
Art	10
Music	9
Video Games	2

    a. How many students in all reported their hobbies in this chart?
    b. Which of these hobbies is the best use of time for students?
    c. What kind of activities do the students enjoy most: physical or artistic?
    d. What is the numeric difference between the most popular and least popular hobby?

54. Which of the following practices is the best use of technology to increase reading comprehension and literacy skills?

    a. Encourage the use of tape recorders in class, by which students can record classroom conversations and lessons to be reviewed during homework and study time.
    b. Accessing a specific website online that shows children how to use graphic organizers for the stories and texts which they are reading in class.
    c. Allowing students who have completed their class work to play games or spend monitored time online.
    d. Asking students to read articles on various comprehension skills and provide a post-test to measure how well they can apply specific skills.

Alex: "Yea...I just wasn't really sure what to write on that part, so I left it blank."

Mrs. Blaine: "Can you tell me now how you felt about the book?"

Alex: "It was alright, I guess. It was pretty good. It was boring at first, but I liked the way it ended."

Mrs. Blaine: "And why is that?"

Alex: "It was cool how the burglar was someone you knew all along; the author gave you clues and stuff throughout the story and you could try to solve the mystery while you were reading it."

Mrs. Blaine: "I understand. I liked that part of the story, too. Getting started on work like this can be challenging at first. But it is important that you begin to learn this skill because you will use it over and over again in school and in your eventual career. Let's talk about some ways to help you get going."

Alex: "Okay...sounds good."

69. What skill is Mrs. Blaine referring to in the underlined sentence?
    a. Understanding his feelings.
    b. Completing assignments thoroughly without leaving any information out.
    c. Stating an opinion or thesis and supplying supporting evidence.
    d. Writing even when you are unsure about the topic or instructions.

70. What would be the best way for Mrs. Blaine to help Alex build his skills in this area?
    a. Have Alex write his opinions and each supporting idea on paper plates or pieces of cardstock and show him how to move them around and arrange them in logical order on a large table or the floor.
    b. Have Alex explain his opinions and supporting ideas to her while she writes them down for him; he can then re-write them into the body of his report.
    c. Have Alex participate in extra lessons that let him explore his feelings about or reactions to various media, including books.
    d. Have Alex review each assignment with her before he turns it in to ensure that he has not left anything out.

71. Mr. Benton is in the process of grading the first writing assignments of the year for his eighth-grade students. He is a bit overwhelmed at the volume of errors in grammar, usage and overall composition he finds in almost every student's writing. Mr. Benton wants to use a systematic approach to building his students' writing skills, beginning by giving the students a clear and simple method to apply to their work. His goal is that the students can take part in analyzing and monitoring their own progress. What should he do?

a. Show his students an outline of the six common writing traits and ask the students to evaluate their own skills within each trait. Teacher and student can use this evaluation to establish a plan for working on the skills that need the most help.

b. Assign each student a writing buddy. The students can meet during writing assignments to edit one another's work. They can then separate to make the suggested revisions.

c. Encourage the students to grade their own work using a rubric provided to them. Meet with the student to determine where they believe they need the most help and focus class work around those areas.

d. Teach the students that most writing assignments can be composed using the five-paragraph essay model. Invest class time and homework in perfecting the model that includes thesis, evidence, and conclusions.

72. Mrs. Matson's 6th graders are chatting during snack time and she overhears the following conversation:

Ellie: I hate how my mom always asks me how my day was, every single day! And then she gets mad when I say it's fine. But it really IS fine almost every day!
Brynn: Oh, I know! My dad always wants to know what my reading is about, but sometimes I just don't feel like talking about it. It takes long enough to read it without talking about it.
Jon: You have it easy. My mom AND dad help me with my homework every night, and then they give me extra work to do!

Mrs. Matson would like to not only give students a chance to voice their feelings about the changing communications with their parents, but also help them find a way to channel those feelings into something positive. Which project would be best for allowing students a positive way to communicate with their parents about what is happening in school?

a. Encourage the students to talk to their parents about everything that is happening in school; after all, their parents only want to help them.

b. After talking about this issue, ask the students to write short pieces about their schoolwork and experiences during the day and compile them into a newsletter to be sent home every two weeks.

c. Help the students write letters to their parents, telling them how they feel about the issue

d. Tell students to keep a log of their activities in the classroom and throughout the day to be shown to parents on a daily or weekly basis.

73. A middle-school teacher has written several questions on the chalk board to assist students in revising their most recent essays.

> Do you know the meanings of all the vocabulary in your essay?
> Did you use any major words (besides articles like a, an, and, the) more than three times?
> Do you like the way your writing sounds when you read it aloud?
> Does all the language used make sense?

Judging by the questions above, which writing trait is this teacher encouraging her students to work on today?

  a. sentence fluency
  b. ideas and development
  c. writing conventions
  d. word choice

74. Read the persuasive writing excerpt below:

> "Why Peace is Important"
> Peace is important to our lives. We have to have peace because we can't be fighting all the time. When people fight, they can't do anything else. It also makes everybody else feel upset and angry because they have to listen to the fighting. If you want to have peace you can talk to the person and try to get them to agree with you and say you are sorry if you do something wrong.

How could a teacher help this student develop his persuasive writing skills, based on this initial attempt?

  a. Continue to give positive reinforcement; this student has a good understanding of the persuasive structure.
  b. Introduce the use of a graphic organizer or flow chart to help the student organize his main idea and supporting evidence in a logical way.
  c. Encourage the student to include more details in his writing to make it more interesting and more personal.
  d. Focus primarily on the editing and revising processes to correct writing conventions, usage, and grammar.

75. A Language teacher is introducing a new writing topic to her class. She asks them to pretend that the person they are writing to or for is "an alien from outer space." What type of writing is she probably introducing?

  a. Fantasy/fiction
  b. Poetry
  c. Persuasive essay
  d. How-to article

76. Ms. Burns' fourth-graders are working very hard at building writing skills on many levels. They have come a long way with their knowledge of the six traits of writing, as well as their confidence in their own abilities. Some of the students have trouble finding their own unique "voices" when writing, probably because they are working so hard to maintain accurate grammar, spelling, organization, and continuity of ideas. How can Ms. Burns help the students inject their own personalities and voices into their writing without sacrificing correctness?

a. Explain that they should always be sure to include personal opinions and insights to make the writing interesting.

b. Project overhead examples of good writing that appropriately utilizes personal voice and lead a discussion about them in class.

c. Guide students to select only topics with which they are very knowledgeable and explain that it is never a good idea to write about something that is unfamiliar to them.

d. Teach students to imagine themselves as a new character every time they write--they should write from the point of view of that individual, phrasing things the way that person or character would if they were speaking.

77. Read the excerpt below:

I like sweets. Cookies, cake and ice cream are very sweet and good. I like to eat these things after school or after I eat. Sweet tastes are the best for me and I do not like salty food. When I eat dessert, I feel so good and happy. My mom says that I should not eat too many sweets or I will get cavities, so I have to brush my teeth after eating them.

Which activity would benefit this student's writing skills the most?

a. Make "word bulletin boards" with the student to help her build vocabulary to make her writing more interesting.

b. Practice with editing other students' writing to familiarize her with writing conventions.

c. Grammar exercises, specifically subject-verb agreement.

d. Encouraging her to select a more challenging writing topic to stretch her skill level.

78. Mr. Talbot's class has an opportunity to begin writing letters to students in France who are learning English, just as Mr. Talbot's class is learning French. He knows that this will be an excellent opportunity for the students to work on letter-writing as well as build their language skills. What other writing skill can he use this opportunity to strengthen in his students?

a. He can help them work through the five-step writing process and the six traits of writing; letter-writing is an excellent exercise for bringing all of those traits and steps together.

b. He can teach them the proper formatting of letters and the etiquette of writing a good letter.

c. He can teach them to consider their audience when writing by talking about what they know of their pen pals' lives, what they would find interesting, and how to communicate effectively with others who are not like themselves.

d. He can teach his students about the importance of proper writing conventions like punctuation, grammar, and spelling, because their pen pals are still learning English.

85. Mrs. Gilbert, an English teacher, and Ms. Dudley, an Art teacher, are working together to create an integrated unit of study for their common students. The students will be studying King Tut, reading various accounts of his life, both fiction and non-fiction. Ms. Dudley will be guiding the students through various art projects related to the time period in which King Tut lived (e.g., making papyrus). Which choice provides an example of an additional project or lesson that will address visual interpretation and decoding skills?

a. The students participate in Ancient Egypt Day and can dress up as characters or historical figures from the appropriate time period.

b. The students visit a local museum exhibit on Ancient Egypt and keep a log of visual images and representations they see. The class discusses those images and their meanings during both classes.

c. The students write stories about the lives of Ancient Egyptians and draw illustrations to go along with their writing.

d. The students watch a movie about King Tut and create free-writing pieces based on what they have seen.

86. Mrs. Canas has had a parent offer to visit her fifth-grade class and provide a sign language seminar. The parent is fluent in American Sign Language and would like to offer her skills to benefit the students. Mrs. Canas thinks the seminar will be very interesting and provide a unique way to hone her students' listening and expressive skills. Which choice identifies another language skill set that would indirectly benefit from this seminar?

a. Students' understanding of how visual messages, including body language, facial expression, and signs inform verbal communication and ideas.

b. Students' fine motor skills and hand-eye coordination.

c. Students' respect for other cultures, specifically the non-hearing community.

d. Students' ability to communicate with other peers and adults in their community.

87. An eighth-grade class will be watching a mystery film in English class over the next two days. Throughout the story, the camera will often focus on objects or clothing that are colored bright red. These objects are always related to clues that lead the character toward solving the mystery. What literary device is the students' teacher planning to introduce in this context?

a. Media deconstruction

b. Color imagery

c. Alliteration

d. Symbolism

88. Middle school students at Ms. Kelso's school are expected to complete a large independent study project to be presented at the end of the second term. The project is the culmination of reading research, writing a paper, and the final element of publishing, or presentation. The students can choose how they present their work and are instructed to use visual aids. Which of the following would be a helpful guideline for Ms. Kelso to offer her students?

a. Whenever possible, use pictures, video, music, charts and graphs to supplement your presentation for the purpose of keeping your audience's interest.

b. Think about any parts of your paper that might be hard to explain. Choose a visual aid to help you show your audience the concept, and then use your words to explain it.

c. Select the most interesting photographs from your research, create color photocopies, and pass them throughout the class during your presentation.

d. Use your main ideas and supporting evidence to create a Power-point slideshow, making note-taking and organization simple and clear.

89. Which of the following visual images would be most appropriate for teaching students about how media images influence their perceptions and attitudes?

    a. a photograph found in a journalistic magazine, such as Time
    b. an illustration or diagram found in the students' own Social Studies textbook
    c. a political cartoon found in the newspaper
    d. a non-political cartoon found in another section of the newspaper

Use the following information to answer questions 90 and 91:

> A middle school class is working through the process of creating a research project. Since this kind of assignment is completely new, their teacher provides direct instruction and practice assignments to help the students approach the large project.

90. Which of the following approaches would increase a middle-school student's preliminary research skills?

    a. Assign and analyze a research paper on a topic of the student's choosing.
    b. Require students to submit a separate outline before completing a research paper.
    c. Require students to turn in note cards containing relevant information on each source they will use in an upcoming research project.
    d. Pre-test on several subjects to determine which area or discipline to explore.

91. What is the first point at which the teacher should meet individually to talk with the student?

    a. After the student first chooses a topic
    b. After the student turns in research note cards
    c. After the student completes the initial outline
    d. After the rough draft has been turned in

92. An eighth-grade teacher notices that her students perform very well on scheduled tests in class, but struggle with pop quizzes or other in-class assignments that involve recalling information. In discussing this issue with other teachers on her team, she finds that this is a pattern across all disciplines. What would be the best way to help students retain information on a daily or weekly basis in the absence of the motivation of an upcoming test?

    a. Devote the first few minutes of class on previewing information and tasks and the last few minutes of each class summarizing highlights from class work and homework reading.
    b. Increase the frequency of pop quizzes in hopes that the students will begin to study at home more often.
    c. Give the students a study guide before each quiz so they know what will be tested.
    d. Allow the students to work on the quizzes in groups so that they can help each other with memory and recall.

necessary language skills. In Choice "d", students practice listening skills, which would only indirectly build oral skills. Choice "b" allows students to learn not only by listening, but by having a chance to explain or assist when he or she has the requisite skills to do so. A skilled student is also there to assist when needed.

6. D: The "Phrase of the Day" appears from the question prompt to be dedicated to certain types of oral language, including analogies and idioms. By asking the students to record interpretations in an informal way (through pictures or the students' own words), he will have insight as to their perceptions about common language. He also directly builds the students' oral language skills by giving them the correct meaning of the phrase with which the students can compare their original answers. In this way, Mr. Campbell assesses and builds skills without the use of a formal test or quiz.

7. B: Oral language skills incorporate speaking, listening, and knowledge of conventional language. In Choice "a", students would be limited to a very specific vocabulary in order to work with the science and math programs, and would not have opportunities to increase their knowledge of language. In Choice "c", students are practicing their listening skills, but are not required to speak or think critically about what they have heard. Choice "d" does involve technology and class discussions; however, the benefit of watching the discussion on tape is relatively unclear. In Choice "b", students not only have a chance to build their speaking and listening skills, but also increase their knowledge of other cultures and ways of speaking.

8. C: In choices "a" and "b," students are primarily using written language in order to present to the class. They are required to use what they have composed as the text for their oral presentations. In Choice "c", students have the chance to learn how to prioritize information they have read and written, and also learn to modify the written word to create an oral presentation based upon specific parameters. This exercise highlights the differences between the written and spoken word. Choice "d" does not necessarily involve all of the students and less directly increases the students' oral skills in a relevant way.

9. D: In this activity, students are practicing a variety of skills related to communication. By analyzing the log sheet, it is apparent that students are expected to work on their conversational skills, including listening and speaking. Choice "a" refers to those points on the log sheet that relate to listening while another person is speaking. Choice "c" also pertains to listening skills, specifically with eye contact and other behaviors that let the student know that his partner was listening and making an effort to understand. Choice "b" refers to the ability to speak clearly (each word can be clearly understood) and effectively (the ideas behind the words make sense to the listener). Choice "d" could potentially come to fruition; however, conflict resolution is not specifically addressed in this activity.

10. C: Oral language skills are almost un-quantifiable because they cover a multitude of competencies. Vocabulary, enunciation, listening, body language, comprehension and many other skills directly affect a student's communicative ability. This particular activity primarily focuses on peer interactions. However, conversing with adults provides opportunities for students to learn new vocabulary and ways of speaking. Choices "a," " b" and "d" are possible outcomes or functions of the teacher's partnering with a new student during each conversation. However, teachers must keep in mind that it is just as important for students to converse with adults in a context that allows them to learn from observation as well as participation.

11. D: In the debate process, it is important for students to take a position and support it with evidence or arguments in order to make their claims effective. Choice "d" requires students to formulate their opinions and supporting arguments, and helps them reduce extraneous information and create "reminders" for their talking points on notecards. Choice "c" requires students to prepare their arguments but encourages reading aloud during the debate rather than actually speaking directly to their opponent or to the crowd. Choice "c" fails to help students distinguish between written language and oral language and their occasionally separate purposes. Choice "b" creates opportunities for informal debate, but does not teach students the parameters for formal debating. Choice "a" is similarly informal and does not familiarize students with the preparation process with respect to formulating arguments, opinions, or preparing to speak in front of a large audience.

12. A: In Choice "a", the teacher guides previewing of information to show students how to put themselves in the right frame of mind to listen carefully for meaning. Students are then able to listen in a guided way based upon the previewing. By varying the type of comprehension assessment, the teacher will get a better understanding of what the students learned. Choice "b" is a good exercise, but does not provide for direct instruction by the teacher or a particularly skilled student. In Choice "c", students are focusing more upon reading comprehension than listening since they must read the story to themselves and then write a report. There is then no way to gauge what they have learned. The final choice would be useful, but does not include teacher-guided previewing, which is very helpful in building comprehension.

13. B: At the start of a new school year, a teacher will likely choose to engage in a series of exercises to help her understand her students' current ability levels. These exercises must provide opportunities for evaluation of the whole class, rather than a select few students. In Choice "a", the teacher is not likely to get a lot of information from each student during class discussion, since not all children may participate. An instruction-level text may also prove too difficult for some students to read without guidance from a fluent reader. Choice "c", while a good exercise for peer-assisted reading, would not provide the teacher chances to evaluate each student's comprehension at once. Choice "d" would be very time-consuming; it would also cause students to influence each other's comprehension (e.g. the students going first may influence the comprehension of those re-telling the story later). Choice "b" allows the teacher to evaluate the students' independent comprehension levels with one assignment.

14. A: Emergent readers are those who are not yet reading fluently (with appropriate speed and accuracy). Choice "b" refers to the practice of reviewing relationships between letters and sounds, which is vital to building reading skills. Choice "c" would help students build vocabulary retention by requiring them to find unfamiliar words in the dictionary. This practice causes the student to analyze and retain spelling of unfamiliar words, as well as reinforces dictionary/reference skills. Choice "d" addresses the fact that many words in the English language are irregularly spelled and cannot be decoded with conventional phonetic instruction. While invented spelling described in Choice "a" may be permitted in emergent readers, this practice is not likely to build specific reading skills.

15. C: Literacy skills encompass a variety of contexts: written, verbal, comprehension, vocabulary, grammar, spelling, etc. Designing class work that touches on these multiple contexts must allow the children to increase not only skills that can be measured on tests or written work. Reading a play gives students a chance to touch on comprehension, vocabulary, and grammar; acting the play out creates the opportunity for increased comprehension and oral interpretation. Each of the alternate answers focuses on one specific aspect of literacy skills, without incorporating multiple contexts.

16. B: Assessment is an ongoing process that involves formal testing and a host of other methods. Students are working at any given time in the school year on a multitude of skills sets, and all of these skills are interrelated and developing simultaneously at different rates. It is impossible to ever provide a "snapshot" of a student's abilities, because each student develops in a unique and complex manner. Choice "a" would only offer insight into a student's reading fluency. Choice "c" would show how a student could perform on standardized tests; however, many factors such as anxiety and test-taking speed affect those scores. Choice "d" relies on the teacher to interpret the student's strengths and weaknesses and would require an almost impossible attention to detail. Choice "b" includes both formal and informal assessments as well as giving insight into writing, vocabulary and other skill sets in a comprehensive portfolio.

17. A: Those who are familiar with the guided oral reading strategy will note that the struggling student must be paired with a fluent and skilled partner. If you are not familiar with this strategy, all of the answer choices could conceivably be a part of the oral reading strategy and appear to be related to one another. However, one choice does not make sense after reading all four options. In answer choices "b" and "d," Valeria's partner is required to read the text aloud and offer correction or feedback when Valeria reads aloud. If Valeria is paired with another struggling student (as suggested in Choice "a", neither "b" nor "d" would prove effective in building her reading fluency.

18. B: Mr. Waleran's purpose is to encourage students to express themselves in written words, interpreting their thoughts into writing. However, there are often children who cannot write well enough to create coherent or legible works. In these cases, it is still possible for students to express themselves in writing. Choice "b" allows Dimitri to express himself by drawing, which will likely make him feel more comfortable with the activity. He will also have the chance to use words he does know and incorporate them into his work. As his skills grow, he can gradually transition into more formal writing. Choices "a" and "c" allow Dimitri to explore his thoughts, but do not build his writing skills. Choice "d" will, in all likelihood, become a chore for Dimitri and reinforce his struggles with reading and writing.

19. D: Part of building literacy skills is showing students how to listen effectively to various types of texts: narrative, poetry, informative, etc. In order to become competent in a variety of literacy skills, students must be able to listen for information and for pleasure/experience. This teacher is not only exposing them to poetry, but creating a forum in which they can actively listen and then discuss what they have experienced or learned. The scenario given in Choice "a" could possibly be true, as could Choice "c". But it is less likely that the teacher would devote an entire month of reading and listening to a specific type of text simply to give her students a break or to make a point about poetry versus prose. Choice "b" assumes that the poetry she reads will rhyme, which is not always the case.

20. B: Mrs. Taylor's project introduces students to an ancient form of expression that was written, but not based upon alphabetic principles, like English. This project is applicable to all levels of readers, as it incorporates various kinds of media to assist comprehension. Students are required to listen and read for information so that they can apply what they have learned to creating their own hieroglyphics. In Choice "b", the answer suggests that what is learned about hieroglyphics will assist students in understanding those with different backgrounds. However, hieroglyphics are not used in any widespread way today, and are much less helpful in building multicultural awareness than perhaps a lesson on modern Egyptian culture or writing.

21. D: Teachers should try to avoid shallow notions of what it means to provide cultural or multi-cultural education; in Choice "a", we cannot presume to understand another person by listening to his favorite music or watching a favorite movie. In Choice "b", there is also the assumption that there is a variety of musical tastes in the class, which may not be the case. In fact, if many students pick the same song, it is possible to use that choice to open up dialogue about what they lyrics mean and why they are so popular with the class. Choice "c" is posed in direct opposition to Choice "d". However, Choice "d" suggests what most teachers know to be true: literacy skills are not just important for schoolwork and class work; students must be able to take meaning from a variety of different sources in order to grow into educated adults. Music is an important medium through which students can express themselves and learn about the world around them through comprehension and listening skills.

22. C: All children learn their letter-sound correspondences at different rates. This particular child may simply be showing his teacher that he has not quite mastered this skill set yet. However, the inconsistence with producing the sounds could possibly be a signal that he needs specialized instruction. It is impossible, however, to know exactly what is going on without providing specialized instruction and giving that instruction time to improve skills. Choice "a" suggests an immediate referral for special-needs testing, which may be unnecessary and too soon in this scenario. Choice "b" states that all children learn differently which is certainly true, but does not provide a plan for helping the child improve. In the final choice, the parents may become needlessly alarmed and spend extra money in a situation where the intervention may not be necessary or even helpful. Choice "c" provides specific instruction in the deficient skill and acknowledges that the child may improve on his own; but if he needs it, extra help can be found.

23. D: Students are expected to be able to express themselves verbally and build upon one another's ideas in class as they complete fourth and fifth grades. However, many students lack the confidence or skills to participate in class discussions or conversations. Rather than leave those students to their own devices, as suggested in choices "a" and "b" a teacher must help instruct the students on how to communicate orally in situations where they can be successful. Choice "c" would require the students to speak out more, but might not alleviate issues with preparedness or confidence as would Choice "d" which allows students to feel more comfortable and get the teacher's guidance.

24. B: This prompt focuses not only on reading fluency skills, but also on the issue of the young reader's confidence. It is very common for students who feel unsuccessful at reading to avoid the skill altogether. The teacher in this question realizes something important: it is vital to build a student's confidence with reading as he or she builds skill. In choice "a" there is a faulty assumption that a student could ever memorize enough words to eliminate the need to decode. While some students with processing disorders or different learning styles do rely more heavily on sight words, this practice should not be solely relied upon. In choice "c" the students will likely feel negatively about being asked to read young children's books; their lack of confidence may be reinforced by this plan. In choice "d" students may also be frustrated by the extra work they are required to do without any evidence of success with this practice. In Choice "b", students can build their fluency skills by creating words with various sounds, which is often easier for students than decoding as they are learning to read. As their knowledge of letter-sound relationships grows, they will become better at decoding words they see on the page. Allowing students to encode will also provide them with more chances to feel successful as they learn.

25. C: Reading fluency is defined as a set of skills including speed, accuracy and inflection when reading words on a page. Reading comprehension generally refers to the ability to understand what is being read. Both sets of skills are important, and reading fluency is vital to comprehension, which is the ultimate goal of the practice of reading. It is possible, even common, to isolate skills for the purpose of skill-building or to compensate for areas in which a student is struggling; however, all skills are inter-related. Children can make progress in some aspects of reading while still working on more difficult areas. Based on these ideas, choices "a" and "d" can be ruled out as possible answers. Comprehension is typically not classified as being part of fluency skills, which eliminates

Alex, like many students, is not confident in his ability to clearly state an idea and back it up with supporting evidence or ideas from what he has read. This is the skill she is suggesting he will need to use again and again. Alex has an opinion, that the book was "boring at first," but he "liked the way it ended." He knows how he feels about the book, but does not know how to explain his opinion in writing. Therefore, answer Choice "a" is inaccurate. Choices "b" and "c" are both likely to be necessary for Alex at some point, but are unlikely to be the most important skill Mrs. Blaine mentions.

70. A: Alex is having trouble expressing a logical argument in writing. However, he has an opinion about the book to get him started. By having him write each idea on separate items, Alex can use tangible objects to represent his thoughts. He can then move them around as he thinks through how they are related to one another. In this way, he can start to structure his thoughts with the help of visual aids, rather than attempting to do this abstractly. The remaining three choices might assist Alex with certain assignments, but will not give him concrete tools to help him organize his thoughts and write them in a clear, concise way.

71. A: Mr. Benton wants to use a clear-cut approach to writing, involving students in the process. As a teacher, Mr. Benton should know that there are six commonly agreed-upon writing traits: idea development, organization, voice, word choice, sentence fluency and conventions. These traits encompass the majority of writing skills that students will learn over the course of their studies. In Choice "a", not only does Mr. Benton provide students with this framework for thinking about writing, but helps them prioritize their needs in building their skills. The students can then work from the plan devised from that initial meeting. In choices "b" and "c", students are left primarily to their own devices to build their writing skills. However, if most of the students are struggling with writing (as suggested in the question prompt), it would not be advisable to leave the writing instruction to the students themselves. Choice "d" provides faulty information--there are many types of writing that would not be written in the five-paragraph style or format.

72. B: Part of teaching older students is helping them give voice to what is happening in their lives and connecting that voice to what they are learning in class. In Choice "b", students not only have a voice, but can channel that voice into a particular type of writing. In this case, they will be writing journalistically. They also have a chance to turn their frustration into a positive activity that will give parents the information they would like to know. In Choice "a", the students do not build any particular writing skills, nor does the problem get solved for parents or students. In Choice "c", the students would have a chance to write about their feelings, but this does not eliminate the issue of parents wanting to know what is happening at school. Choice "d" only serves to make more work for the students, without building their writing skills.

73. D: The first two questions suggest that the primary focus of this exercise is word choice and vocabulary. The third question refers to the sound of the words chosen, and could also pertain to Choice "a", sentence fluency. The fourth question would work with choices "a," "c" or "d". But taken together, the questions point strongly to the concept of word choice. Choice "a", sentence fluency, refers to the way the words in sentences work together. Choice "b" refers to the way the students' ideas are developed in the paper. Choice "c" encompasses writing conventions such as punctuation, spacing, and capitalization.

74. B: In persuasive writing, the writer must introduce an opinion or statement about which he or she must provide supporting evidence. The paragraph or paper should start with the main idea and then segue into separate but related supporting details. In this writing sample, the student's ideas are written sequentially, as the student might think about them mentally. Introducing a visual aid to help him separate his primary idea and the ideas that give reasons for it may help him develop the

135

piece into a longer, more logical argument. He already includes personal details and ideas that make the piece interesting to read, contrary to Choice "c". Choice "d" suggests that the student may have many grammatical and conventional corrections to make, which is not correct. While it is always important to encourage, as stated in Choice "a", Choice "b" would be the most direct, concrete way to assist this student in developing his skills.

75. D: When teachers talk to their students about writing, it is important to remember that young writers often leave out important details or information vital to its coherence. Students must learn to communicate clearly through writing and include all pertinent information. The teacher uses the metaphor of the alien from outer space to emphasize this point—an alien would have no prior knowledge that would aid comprehension, therefore the writer must be very thorough. This concept is important in all writing, but would be especially important in explaining to another person how to do something. In Choice "d", a student would choose a favorite activity, sport, or task and explain in a methodical way how to complete or participate in it. Neglecting any piece of information would make the piece irrelevant.

76. B: Many aspects of writing are difficult to teach directly. There are not as many specific exercises that show students how to write in their own voices without being overly colloquial or even incorrect. Students must always be working toward adhering to writing conventions, but also making that which they write personal and interesting. Part of "voice" is personal expression and making writing relevant to the intended audience. Often, the best way to show the students how to do this is to show them that which has already been done well and discuss why the writing is good. The students can use this discussion to improve their own writing through emulation. Choice "a" suggests that personal opinions are always relevant to one's writing, which is not always the case, depending on the type of assignment. In Choice "c", students would be very limited should they only choose subjects with which they are familiar--they would rarely have a chance to grow. The final choice would encourage students to speak in someone else's voice, which would create variety, but would not grow their ability to speak as themselves in any relevant or interesting way.

77. A: Reading this excerpt, it becomes apparent that the student is using a limited writing vocabulary. The words "sweet" or "sweets" are used three times; "like" is used three times as well. The sentences feel very repetitive because many words are used again and again. Working with students to build their vocabulary is one of the most helpful ways to build writing skills. The more words in a student's repertoire, the more interesting and lively his writing will be. Despite the vocabulary deficit, the student's writing conventions and grammar are actually quite good in this excerpt. Choice "d" suggests that the student needs to stretch his writing skill by choosing more challenging topics, but we do not know from this piece whether or not the student is working at an appropriate level of challenge.

78. C: Choice "a" is misleading, as writing a letter is a specific format and kind of exercise; it is not typically considered a catch-all exercise for learning the five-step process or the six traits of writing. While every writing exercise can be a backdrop for these skills, Choice "a" is not the most accurate answer. If you read the question prompt carefully, you see that it is already acknowledged that this opportunity will be a good exercise for showing students how to write a letter well. Therefore, Choice "b" is redundant. Choice "d" is true; students should be careful of their writing conventions so that their writing is easier to read, yet Choice "c" is the skill than can be most directly applied when writing to students of another language and culture; the audience actually encompasses Choice "d", as students would determine in thinking about their French pen pals that they might have a hard time reading English, and that they should be cognizant of that fact.

79. B: By the eighth grade, students should begin to understand the purposes and effectiveness of various media. If the students have been learning about how to deconstruct media messages, they have likely been studying ideas about audience, point of view, and persuasive language. Assigning a project in which the students are guided to think through these concepts will solidify their understanding of how media messages are created. Each of the other answers, "a," "b" and "d" will likely be accomplished through the completion of this project. However, it is not likely that the teacher has designed such a specific kind of assignment in order to increase her students' real-life job skills, as not all of them will go into media-related fields described in Choice "a". Choice "c" assumes that technology will be used in the assignment, although it is possible for students to create the ads and essays without the use of computers or other technology. Choice "d" could be accomplished by any number of assignments and is less likely to be the primary intended outcome.

80. A: Inkblot images are often used to gain insight into an individual's thoughts. The teacher clearly understands that different people will interpret these images in various ways. She asks the students to write their questions down so that they will not be influenced by others' interpretations. While some visual symbols are universal, most images are not inherent as suggested in Choice "b". Choice "c" could possibly be true, but would be irrelevant to a group of sixth graders in most circumstances. Choice "d" supposes that students should confer with one another before forming their own opinions, which should not be a rule of thumb. By allowing students to interpret the messages individually and then share their perceptions, the teacher will demonstrate that the individual's point of view will affect his understanding of visual images.

81. D: Students typically enjoy watching film versions of literature, especially when the text is challenging to read. An important part of media consumption is building skills to deconstruct the embedded ideas and messages. The teacher in this scenario wants the students to think about how the structure and content of the film affects their understanding of a classic story. In choices "a" and "b", students are assigned to state their opinions about certain aspects of the film or play, but are not asked to critically analyze a specific message. Choice "c" simply creates a rather tedious assignment that will yield a rote list of examples. Choice "d" targets the unique setting of the film and encourages students to think about why the film's creators might have chosen to adapt the story in such a way, which is likely to suggest that the content of the story is relevant to people in any era or setting.

82. A: Mr. James is showing students the difference between a main idea (or concept) and its supporting evidence (or details). He has taken an element of a story and provided three details or character traits that provide proof of his claim. The organization of the graph helps students see the relationship between in the ideas, in addition to hearing it. This skill can be directly applied to either constructing meaning from a text or creating a well-planned paragraph. Choice "b" may not always be true, depending on the kind of questions asked. Choice "c" assumes that characters in texts can always be broken down into smaller components. Choice "d" refers to aspects of writing such as punctuation, grammar, spelling, etc.

83. B: Students are expected to have a variety of skills with respect to viewing, representing, and analyzing visual/media images by the time they enter high school. They should be able to understand visual imagery and how it affects or creates meaning. Students must also learn to deconstruct the messages they see and create their own for the purposes of communicating their own ideas. Choice "a" would, perhaps, be the goal of a consumerism or economics class, but is not the best choice for this scenario. This game would create understanding in students about different types of visual images, but they are not likely to be the same images used in their schoolwork at this juncture. Choice "d" is certainly true; the children will likely enjoy the game. However, Choice "b" most closely matches the educational requirements and standards laid out for students of this age.

84. D: Generally speaking, the following story elements take place in sequential order:

Exposition: refers to background information and actions in a story that describe the setting, characters, etc.

Rising action: events in the plot that lead up to the critical event or turning point

Climax: critical event, dramatic scene, or turning point in the story

Falling action: resulting events and actions following the conflict

Resolution: all actions and events are resolved and addressed

Teaching students about the plot elements they can find in most stories will help them develop many skills, including comparisons/contrasts, plot analysis, reading comprehension, etc.

85. B: Ancient Egypt provides a rich backdrop for a myriad of literacy skills. Students can develop their visual literacy skills in a number of ways, even using material and studies that date back thousands of years. In Choice "a", students are creating visual images with costume and dress, but no method for decoding those messages is stated in the answer choice. Drawing illustrations focuses on the same skill: creation of visual images, but no decoding or discussion of those images. In Choice "d", students could build their visual literacy skills if they were to discuss the visual images or representations in the film, but this activity is not included in the answer choice. In the correct answer, B), students are exposed to various representations and exhibits regarding the material in question and then have a chance to discuss and uncover meaning in what they have seen, with the guidance of the teachers.

86. A: If you read the question prompt carefully, you will notice that the question refers specifically to language skills. While Choice "c" is important and would likely result from the exercise, it does not signify a specific language skill. Students' motor skills are not likely to significantly improve over the course of one day, eliminating Choice "b". In Choice "d", the assumption that other individuals in the community would be able to interpret sign language is incorrect. But the seminar would indeed provide an opportunity for students to learn about how visual representations affect meaning. Using sign language allows them to hone listening and expression skills simultaneously, as well as to learn how to decode non-verbal expressions.

87. D: In literature and in media, storytellers often use the color red to symbolize a number of concepts: red can signal importance, danger, love, or simply draw the viewer or reader to the particular object in question. The question prompt tells you directly that the red objects signify that the main character is seeing a clue to solving the mystery. In essence, anything colored red represents, or symbolizes, a clue.

88. B: The primary purpose of visual aids is to extend or enhance meaning. Visuals can sometimes distract from the meaning of the presentation if used too much, as in Choice "a". Choice "c" could also create distractions in that students may be more likely to look at photos directly in front of them than pay attention to the student presenting. The final choice simply encourages students to read the information on screen, and will likely cause the presenting student to read aloud rather than communicate in his own words. Choice "b", however, utilizes the students' thought processes in determining where a visual might help enhance understanding, and requires them to use oral communication as well.

138

89. C: In teaching about this subject, students must be able to understand the intended meaning of a particular media image. To do this, they have to consider the image-creator's background, point of view, and anything else they might be able to determine from analyzing the image. Students need to be taught tools to dissect the barrage of images that they see on a daily basis. Choice "a" encompasses photos of real-life people and events. While these photos are valuable for many teaching purposes, it cannot be guaranteed that students would be able to apply their tools to current-day media analysis. Choice "b" is the choice least related to media influence in that it refers to a Social Studies text, likely created for didactic purposes. Choice "d" most likely refers to a cartoon found in the Funnies, created to entertain, rather than influence. The political cartoon in Choice "c" is the image most explicitly created to affect and influence public opinion by exaggerating personal traits and personalizing lofty issues.

90. C: Many factors affect the final outcome of a research paper or project, including the selection of sources, interpretation of source information, organization of ideas, and writing skills. The final project described in answer "a" is not always indicative of how efficiently a student has researched a topic because it is the end-result of many language processes at work. The outline mentioned in answer "b" would provide insight about the organization of ideas, but answer "c" would allow the instructor to assess the actual process of gathering and synthesizing sources of information.

91. A: One of the most important aspects of completing a research project is topic selection. A student must choose a topic that is appropriately narrow to avoid being overwhelmed by too much information. If the topic is too broad, the student will not be able to adequately research; if it is too narrow, he or she will get stuck. The student should also think critically about whether or not the topic can be researched. For instance, if a student chooses to study a current event, there may not be enough reliable information published yet to support a real research project. The teacher should play an active role in helping the student select a topic, especially on the student's first try.

92. A: The students tend to do well when they know they will be tested; this probably means that they only sit down to study when they are required to do so, unless they want to risk a poor test score. However, it is important for students to retain information each day and week, rather than cramming and memorizing for a test. By devoting a few minutes each day to preview or prepare students for what they will learn, they will begin to learn how to pay attention to the main ideas and salient details of the readings. By reviewing and summarizing, students can compare what they thought would be important during the preview to what they actually learned. The repetition will help the students retain the information from one day to the next.

93. B: If only the first graph was drawn, it may appear that the students were working simply on character analysis or even inferential comprehension. This first set of boxes creates a framework for analyzing and recording information about two specific characters and their personalities. However, taken with the second chart, it becomes apparent that the purpose of the first chart is to organize information in order to complete the second chart. The second chart requires students to think critically about how the two characters are the same and how they are different. This exercise most closely corresponds with Choice "b", comparing and contrasting, in the context of character traits. Choices "c" and "d" are certainly involved in this process, but are simply tools that are used in order to teach students how to compare and contrast

94. B: The question prompt states that the students' primary problems lie in homework: they are concerned about the volume of reading and ho to know what information is most relevant. Although Choice "d" is important and will help students, it will not improve their ability to deal with independent reading and assignments. Choice "c" will help students score more highly on tests, but will likely not improve their study skills. Choice "a" will simply encourage students to "cram' a lot of

139

information for tests. Choice "b", however, teaching SQ3R, is a method by which students can study, internalize and sort through large amounts of information on an independent basis.

95. B: Writing a research paper is a learned skill that begins with proper topic selection. Students must learn to pick topics with guidance from their teachers that can be researched easily. They must be careful not to pick topics that are too broad or too narrow. In this scenario, students also need to pick a topic that can be found as the subject in a variety of sources, including newspapers, magazines, books, etc. Therefore, the topic should be well-known to most readers. Choice "a" is not likely to be found in these sources unless the Velasquez family is nationally, or at least locally, well-known. Choice "c" is probably not appropriate for the same reason. Choice "d" could be considered for an essay topic or another type of writing assignment, but may not be the best choice with respect to the variety of sources. Choice "b" offers a broad subject about which much will have been written.

96. D: The purpose of this kind of note-taking is, on one level, to help students distinguish between major ideas or concepts and the details that support or relate to them. This kind of note-taking also helps students understand how certain events and ideas influence one another. The most important benefit of this practice is that it helps the note-taker start to build meaning out of the information which they receive in class. Students often complain that they don't know how to pick out what will be on a test, or what is important, as they cannot possibly retain every sentence uttered in class. Students do best when they can pick out main ideas and organize their thinking around these concepts, learning details and supporting ideas as they go.

97. C: As is true with students and adults alike, we remember more information when we review it consistently over time. If a student takes meaningful and accurate notes, reviewing them periodically and consistently will help them retain the information and cut down on time spent studying right before the test. This practice also helps the student identify any ideas or questions that need to be addressed before the test or paper is due. Choices "a" and "b" create the impression that a student will struggle if he does not record (in writing or via tape recorder) every word uttered in class. It is more important for students to learn how to create meaning and understand relationships between all of the facts, figures, and concepts introduced in class. Choice "d" would be very time-consuming and would not guarantee that students are choosing the most important ideas and information for use.

98. C: Allowing the students to practice these types of questions starts to open up their ability to show that which they know. Many students experience stress in the transition to various types of testing that do not provide answer choices in multiple choice form, or lack word banks. Choice "c" shows students how to approach these kinds of questions in a safe, un-graded way, and solidifies their thinking by discussing their attempts afterward. Choice "a" may assist with students' recall of information, but does not provide direct instruction on how to formulate answers. Choice "b" will give students time to approach the questions and revise their answers if necessary. For those students who experience more difficulty, however, it may not be as helpful as Choice "c". Choice "d" might also be helpful for any students who experience test anxiety or are taking a bit longer to understand the process, but will not scaffold their attempts as well as Choice "c".

99. C: In a piece of writing such as Sully's, there are two important things which he needs to do; namely, he must select the most important ideas and focus on those, rather than attempt to include every single idea he may have. Once he has done that, he additionally must include details or evidence to support those ideas. Choice "c" gives him a concrete way to identify the most important ideas and match them with appropriate and relevant evidence. Choices "a" and "b" require him to start over on a project, which is unnecessary. Choice "d" would cause him to create a very lengthy and too-detailed report without much focus.

100. B: Studying can be a mystifying experience for students as they begin to do it more frequently. Often, students do not know how to prepare properly for specific kinds of assignments, and direct instruction is helpful. In Choice "b", Mrs. Bray can identify why the students' preparation is not adequate for the examinations and help them understand alternative methods of preparation. In Choice "a", students may or may not improve their performance while taking more quizzes; in fact, their motivation and confidence may decrease if they continue to receive poor grades. Choice "c" contradicts the question prompt, as Mrs. Bray does not want to give the students too many ideas about what will be covered in the quiz; rather, she wants to improve their study skills. Choice "d" is less accurate and direct as a method for achieving her goals than is Choice "b", because parents do not always have good study skills or knowledge of the classroom.

WEST-E Social Studies Practice Test

1. Some countries in the Americas still have large populations of indigenous or partly indigenous peoples. Of the following, which pair of countries does not have comparatively as large of an indigenous population as the other countries?

    a. Guatemala and Peru
    b. Ecuador and Bolivia
    c. Paraguay and Mexico
    d. Argentina and Uruguay

2. Which of the following statements is *not* true regarding English expansionism in the 16th century?

    a. England's defeat of the Spanish Armada in 1588 brought a decisive end to their war with Spain.
    b. King Henry VIII's desire to divorce Catherine of Aragon strengthened English expansionism.
    c. Queen Elizabeth's support for the Protestant Reformation strengthened English expansionism.
    d. Sir Francis Drake and other English sea captains plundered the Spaniards' plunders of Indians.

3. Which of the following is *not* correct regarding the Virginia Companies?

    a. One of these companies, the Virginia Company of Plymouth, made its base in North America.
    b. One of these companies, the Virginia Company of London, made its base in Massachusetts.
    c. One company had a charter to colonize America between the Hudson and Cape Fear rivers.
    d. One company had a charter to colonize America from the Potomac River to north Maine.

4. Which of the following conquistadores unwittingly gave smallpox to the Indians and destroyed the Aztec empire in Mexico?

    a. Balboa
    b. Ponce de Leon
    c. Cortes
    d. De Vaca

5. Which statement best describes the significance of the Peter Zenger trial in colonial America?

    a. It was the earliest American case on the right to bear arms.
    b. It established a precedent for freedom of the press.
    c. It was the earliest American case on right of peaceable assembly.
    d. It established a precedent for freedom of religion.

6. Which of these factors was *not* a direct contributor to the beginning of the American Revolution?

    a. The attitudes of American colonists toward Great Britain following the French and Indian War
    b. The attitudes of leaders in Great Britain toward the American colonies and imperialism
    c. James Otis's court argument against Great Britain's Writs of Assistance as breaking natural law
    d. Lord Grenville's Proclamation of 1763, Sugar Act, Currency Act, and especially Stamp Act

7. Which of the following statements is *not* true regarding the Tea Act of 1773?

   a. The British East India Company was suffering financially because Americans were buying tea smuggled from Holland.

   b. Parliament granted concessions to the British East India Company to ship tea straight to America, bypassing England.

   c. Colonists found that even with added taxes, tea directly shipped by the British East India Company cost less, and they bought it.

   d. American colonists refused to buy less expensive tea from the British East India Company on the principle of taxation.

8. Which of the following is true concerning the formation of new state governments in the new United States of America following freedom from British rule?

   a. By the end of 1777, new constitutions had been created for twelve of the American states.

   b. The states of Connecticut and Massachusetts retained their colonial charters, minus the British parts.

   c. The state of Massachusetts required a special convention for its constitution, setting a good example.

   d. The state of Massachusetts did not formally begin to use its new constitution until 1778.

9. Which of the following is *not* a true statement regarding the Louisiana Purchase?

   a. Jefferson sent a delegation to Paris to endeavor to purchase only the city of New Orleans from Napoleon.

   b. Napoleon, anticipating U.S. intrusions into Louisiana, offered to sell the U.S. the entire Louisiana territory.

   c. The American delegation accepted Napoleon's offer, though they were only authorized to buy New Orleans.

   d. The Louisiana Purchase, once it was completed, increased the territory of the U.S. by 50% overnight.

10. Which of these was *not* a factor that contributed to the duel in which Aaron Burr killed Alexander Hamilton?

   a. Some Federalists who opposed U.S. Western expansion were attempting to organize a movement to secede from the Union.

   b. Alexander Hamilton challenged Aaron Burr to a duel because he objected to U.S. expansion into the West, which Burr supported.

   c. Secessionist Federalists tried to enlist Aaron Burr's support for their cause by backing him in his run for Governor of New York.

   d. Alexander Hamilton was the leader of the group that opposed Aaron Burr's campaign to run for New York Governor.

11. Which of the following did *not* occur during the War of 1812?

   a. Early in the war, the U.S. executed a three-pronged invasion of Canada and succeeded on two of three fronts.

   b. Early in the war, Americans won naval battles against the British, but were soon beaten back by the British.

   c. Admiral Oliver Hazard Perry's fleet defeated the British navy on Lake Erie in September, 1813.

   d. William Henry Harrison invaded Canada and defeated the British and the Indians in the Battle of the Thames.

12. Which of the following was *not* an immediate effect of rapid urban growth in the 1800s?

    a. Poor sanitation conditions in the cities
    b. Epidemics of diseases in the cities
    c. Inadequate police and fire protection
    d. Widespread urban political corruption

13. Which of the following laws was instrumental in spurring westward migration to the Great Plains between 1860 and 1880?

    a. The Homestead Act
    b. The Timber Culture Act
    c. The Desert Land Act
    d. All of these laws were instrumental in spurring westward migration to the Great Plains during that period.

14. What did *not* contribute to ending America's neutrality in World War I?

    a. Germany's declaration of a war zone surrounding the British Isles in February, 1913
    b. Germany's declaration of a war on Russia after Archduke Ferdinand's assassination
    c. Germany's sinking the British ship *Lusitania,* which killed 128 American passengers
    d. Germany's declaration of unrestricted submarine warfare on all ships in the war zone

15. Of the following international diplomatic conferences, which one made US-Soviet differences apparent?

    a. The Potsdam conference
    b. The conference at Yalta
    c. Dumbarton Oaks conference
    d. The Tehran conference

16. Which statement about relations between the Middle East and the US and Europe in the 1950s is *not* correct?

    a. President Nasser of Egypt refused to align with the US in the Cold War.
    b. President Eisenhower removed US funding from the Aswan Dam in 1956.
    c. President Nasser nationalized the Suez Canal, which was owned by England.
    d. In 1956, Egypt attacked Israel, and England and France joined in the war.

17. Of the following, which person or group was *not* instrumental in postwar advancement of civil rights and desegregation during the 1940s and 1950s?

    a. The President
    b. The Supreme Court
    c. The Congress
    d. The NAACP

18. Of the programs enacted by President Lyndon B. Johnson's administration, which was most closely related to John F. Kennedy's legacy?

    a. The Economic Opportunity Act
    b. The Civil Rights Act
    c. The Great Society program
    d. All of these were equally related to JFK's legacy.

19. Which statement regarding US international trade policy in the 1990s is *not* correct?

a. In 1994, the General Agreement on Tariffs and Trade (GATT) was approved by Congress.
b. The GATT was between 57 countries who agreed they would remove or reduce many of their tariffs.
c. The GATT created the World Trade Organization (WTO) to settle international trade differences.
d. The NAFTA (North American Free Trade Agreement), ratified in 1994, had originally been set up by George H.W. Bush's administration.

20. Which statement about factors related to the growth of the US economy between 1945 and 1970 is *not* correct?

a. The Baby Boom's greatly increased birth rates contributed to economic growth during this time.
b. The reduction in military spending after World War II contributed to the stronger US economy.
c. Government programs and growing affluence nearly quadrupled college enrollments in 20 years.
d. Increased mobility and bigger families caused fast suburban expansion, especially in the Sunbelt.

21. Which of the following statements regarding immigration to America during the 1980s is *not* true?

a. Twice as many immigrants came to America during the 1980s than during the 1970s.
b. Latin Americans comprised the largest proportion of immigrants to America in the 1980s.
c. Most immigrants to the US in the 1980s were Latin American, Asian, and Caribbean.
d. The 1986 Immigration Reform and Control Act reduced illegal Mexican immigration.

22. Which is *not* correct regarding black activism during the 1960s?

a. There was a riot in the Los Angeles ghetto of Watts in 1965.
b. There was a riot involving black activists in Newark, New Jersey, after the Watts riot.
c. The Mississippi Freedom Democrats unseated that state's delegation at the convention.
d. There was a riot involving black activists in Detroit, Michigan, after the riot in Watts.

23. What was the earliest written language in Mesopotamia?

a. Sumerian
b. Elamite
c. Akkadian
d. Aramaic

24. During which of these periods were pyramids *not* built in Egypt?

a. The Old Kingdom
b. The Middle Kingdom
c. The New Kingdom
d. The Third Dynasty

25. Which of the following is *not* true about the Crusades?

a. Their purpose was for European rulers to retake the Middle East from Muslims
b. The Crusades succeeded at European kings' goal of reclaiming the "holy land"
c. The Crusades accelerated the already incipient decline of the Byzantine Empire
d. Egypt saw a return as a major Middle Eastern power as a result of the Crusades

26. Which of the following events did *not* contribute to the growth of the Italian Renaissance?

a. The Black Death killed 1/3 of the population of Europe
b. The lower classes benefited from the need for laborers
c. The middle classes developed from a need for services
d. All these events contributed to the Italian Renaissance

27. Which of the following is *not* correct regarding assumptions of mercantilism?

a. The money and the wealth of a nation are identical properties
b. In order to prosper, a nation should try to increase its imports
c. In order to prosper, a nation should try to increase its exports
d. Economic protectionism by national governments is advisable

28. Which of the following is *not* true about the English Civil Wars between 1641 and 1651?

a. These wars all were waged between Royalists and Parliamentarians
b. The outcome of this series of civil wars was victory for Parliament
c. These wars legalized Parliament's consent as requisite to monarchy
d. Two of the wars in this time involved supporters of King Charles I

29. Which of the following choices is/are *not* considered among causes of the French Revolution?

a. Famines causing malnutrition and starvation
b. War debt, Court spending, bad monetary system
c. Resentment against the Catholic Church's rule
d. Resentment against the Protestant Reformation

30. Which statement best describes the role played by the French economy in causing the 1789 French Revolution?

a. France's very large national debt led to heavy tax burdens on the French peasantry.
b. Nearly sixty percent of annual national expenditures financed luxuries for the French nobility.
c. Reforms in the guild system allowed many peasants to rise to the middle class.
d. The king's attempt to curtail free trade led skilled journeymen to rebel against the monarchy.

31. Which of the following statements is accurate regarding the end of the First World War?

a. The Treaty of Versailles brought peace among all countries involved in the war
b. The Treaty of Versailles contained a clause for establishing the United Nations
c. President Woodrow Wilson had proposed forming a coalition of world nations
d. President Wilson succeeded in getting the USA to ratify the League of Nations

32. How did Russia's participation in World War I influence the Russian Revolution?

    a. Civilian suffering and military setbacks served as a catalyst for revolutionary forces.
    b. Nicholas III capitalized on battlefield successes to temporarily silence critics.
    c. The government eased laws banning collective action by factory workers to appease social discontent about the war.
    d. Anti-government protesters temporarily ceased protesting to show patriotism in a difficult war.

33. During the decolonization of the Cold War years, which of the following events occurred chronologically latest?

    a. The Eastern Bloc and Satellite states became independent from the Soviet Union
    b. Canada became totally independent from British Parliament via the Canada Act
    c. The Bahamas, in the Caribbean, became independent from the United Kingdom
    d. The Algerian War ended, and Algeria became independent from France

34. Why was U.S. industrialization confined to the Northeast until after the Civil War?

    a. Because the Civil War delayed the development of water-powered manufacturing
    b. Because the Northeast had faster-running rivers than the rivers found in the South
    c. Because Slater's first cotton mill with horse-drawn production lost so much money
    d. Because the technical innovations for milling textiles had not as yet been invented

35. Which of the following statements is *not* an accurate statement about the Puritans in England?

    a. The Puritans unconditionally gave all their support to the English Reformation
    b. The Puritans saw the Church of England as too much like the Catholic Church
    c. The Puritans became a chief political power because of the English Civil War
    d. The Puritans' clergy mainly departed from the Church of England after 1662

36. Which of the following statements is *not* true about the Gilded Age in America?

    a. The Gilded Age was the era of the "robber barons" in the business world
    b. The Gilded Age got its name from the excesses of the wealthy upper class
    c. The Gilded Age had philanthropy Carnegie called the "Gospel of Wealth"
    d. The Gilded Age is a term whose origins have not been identified clearly

37. Which of the following is *not* true about Democracy and the formation of the United States?

    a. The founding fathers stated in the Constitution that the USA would be a democracy
    b. The Declaration of Independence did not dictate democracy but stated its principles
    c. The United States Constitution stipulated that government be elected by the people
    d. The United States Constitution had terms to protect some, but not all, of the people

38. Which of the following statements does *not* describe the average European diet BEFORE the expansion of trade routes?

    a. Europeans ate for survival, not enjoyment.
    b. They had an abundance of preservatives such as salt that could make food last longer.
    c. Grain-based foods such as porridge and bread were staple meals.
    d. Spices were unavailable.

39. Which of these is true concerning the French Revolution, America, and Europe?

　　a. When France's revolution spread and they went to war with other European countries, George Washington allied with the French.
　　b. During the time period around 1792, American merchants were conducting trading with countries on both sides of the war.
　　c. American traders conducted business with various countries, profiting the most from the British West Indies.
　　d. The Spanish navy retaliated against America for trading with the French by capturing American trading ships.

40. Which group overtook Rome in the mid-600s B.C. and established much of its infrastructure, including sewers, roads, and fortifications, only to be driven out of the city in 509 B.C.?

　　a. Latins.
　　b. Etruscans.
　　c. Greeks.
　　d. Persians.

41. The writers of The Federalist Papers published under the pen name "Publius." Who were the authors?

　　a. James Madison, John Jay, and Alexander Hamilton
　　b. George Washington, Thomas Jefferson, and James Madison
　　c. Alexander Hamilton, Benjamin Franklin, and Thomas Jefferson
　　d. Benjamin Franklin, John Jay, and Thomas Jefferson

42. Social studies education has many practical applications. Which of the following is the most direct application of teaching high school seniors the structure of the U.S. government?

　　a. Knowledge of the fundamentals of federalism
　　b. Informed participation in school elections
　　c. Knowledge of a system of checks and balances
　　d. Informed participation in U.S. political processes

43. The U.S. government is best understood as a federalist government because:

　　a. the legislative branch consists of two representative bodies.
　　b. it is a representative democracy rather than a direct democracy.
　　c. political power is divided between the federal government and the states.
　　d. a national Constitution shapes national legislation.

44. One reason the Articles of Confederation created a weak government was because it limited Congress's ability to do what?

　　a. Declare war
　　b. Conduct a census
　　c. Vote
　　d. Tax

45. The philosophy of the late 17th-18th centuries that influenced the Constitution was from the Age of:

    a. Enlightenment
    b. Empire
    c. Discovery
    d. Industry

46. The votes of how many states were needed to ratify the Constitution?

    a. Five
    b. Ten
    c. Nine
    d. Seven

47. Virginian _____ advocated a stronger central government and was influential at the Constitutional Convention.

    a. Benjamin Franklin
    b. James Madison
    c. George Mason
    d. Robert Yates

48. Power divided between local and central branches of government is a definition of what term?

    a. Bicameralism
    b. Checks and balances
    c. Legislative oversight
    d. Federalism

49. The Senate and the House of Representatives are an example of:

    a. Bicameralism
    b. Checks and balances
    c. Legislative oversight
    d. Federalism

50. The Vice President succeeds the President in case of death, illness or impeachment. What is the order of succession for the next three successors, according to the Presidential Succession Act of 1947?

    a. President Pro Tempore of the Senate, Secretary of State, and Secretary of Defense
    b. Speaker of the House, President Pro Tempore of the Senate, and Secretary of State
    c. President Pro Tempore of the Senate, Speaker of the House, and Secretary of State
    d. Secretary of State, Secretary of Defense, and Speaker of the House

51. The President has the power to veto legislation. How is this power limited?

    I. Congress can override the veto
    II. The President cannot line veto
    III. The President cannot propose legislation

    a. I and III
    b. II only
    c. I and II
    d. I only

52. The civil rights act that outlawed segregation in schools and public places also:

 a. Gave minorities the right to vote
 b. Established women's right to vote
 c. Outlawed unequal voter registration
 d. Provided protection for children

53. Which of the following is a power held only by the federal government?

 a. The power to levy taxes, borrow money, and spend money
 b. The power to award copyrights and patents to people or groups
 c. The power to establish the criteria that qualify a person to vote
 d. The power to ratify proposed amendments to the Constitution

54. Of the following actions, which one requires a three-fourths majority?

 a. State approval of a proposed amendment to the Constitution
 b. Submitting a proposal for an amendment to the Constitution
 c. Ratification for appointments to the Presidency in the Senate
 d. The introduction of charges for an impeachment in the House

55. Which of the following statements is *not* correct about U.S. westward expansion and Manifest Destiny?

 a. The idea that U.S. freedom and values should be shared with, even forced upon, as many people as possible had existed for many years.
 b. The term "Manifest Destiny" and the idea it represented had been used for many years prior to the 1830s.
 c. Many Americans believed that America as a nation should ultimately be extended to include Canada and Mexico.
 d. Increased nationalism after the resolution of the War of 1812 and rapid population growth added to Manifest Destiny.

56. Presidential candidates are eligible for public funding if they raise $5,000 per state in how many states?

 a. Twenty
 b. Ten
 c. Twenty-five
 d. Seventeen

57. What judicial system did America borrow from England?

 a. Due process
 b. Federal law
 c. Commerce law
 d. Common law

58. Which of the following is a possible absolute location for New Orleans?

 a. 30° S, 90° E
 b. 30° N, 90° E
 c. 30° S, 90° W
 d. 30° N, 90° W

59. On which type of map are different countries represented in different colors, with no two adjacent countries sharing a color?

    a. Physical map
    b. Political map
    c. Climate map
    d. Contour map

60. Which of the following statements about the equator is true?

    a. It intersects four continents.
    b. It is to the north of both horse latitudes.
    c. It is located at 0° longitude.
    d. It is not very windy.

61. The apparent distance between Greenland and Norway is greatest on a(n)

    a. Mercator Map.
    b. Conic Projection Map.
    c. Contour Map.
    d. Equal-Area Projection Map.

62. Which of the following is *not* a method of representing relief on a physical map?

    a. Symbols
    b. Color
    c. Shading
    d. Contour Lines

63. Which map describes the movement of people, trends, or materials across a physical area?

    a. Political Map
    b. Cartogram
    c. Qualitative Map
    d. Flow-line Map

64. What is the most common type of volcano on earth?

    a. Lava dome
    b. Composite volcano
    c. Shield volcano
    d. Cinder cone

65. Water is continuously recycled in the hydrosphere. By which process does water return to the atmosphere after precipitation?

    a. Percolation
    b. Cohesion
    c. Evaporation
    d. Condensation

66. Which type of rock is formed by extreme heat and pressure?

    a. Limestone
    b. Metamorphic
    c. Sedimentary
    d. Igneous

67. Which part of a hurricane features the strongest winds and greatest rainfall?

    a. Eye wall
    b. Front
    c. Eye
    d. Outward spiral

68. Which of the following are not included in a geographical definition of Southeast Asia?

    a. Myanmar, Laos, Cambodia, and Thailand
    b. Vietnam, the Malay Peninsula, and Brunei
    c. East Malaysia, Indonesia, and the Philippines
    d. These are all geographical parts of Southeast Asia

69. Which of the following exemplifies the multiplier effect of large cities?

    a. The presence of specialized equipment for an industry attracts even more business.
    b. The large population lowers the price of goods.
    c. Public transportation means more people can commute to work.
    d. A local newspaper can afford to give away the Sunday edition.

70. For thousands of years, Africans have cultivated the grasslands south of the Sahara Desert, an area known as the

    a. Qattara Depression.
    b. Great Rift Valley.
    c. Congo Basin.
    d. Sahel.

71. Tracy needs to determine the shortest route between Lima and Lisbon. Which of the following maps should she use?

    a. Azimuthal projection with the North Pole at the center
    b. Azimuthal projection with Lisbon at the center
    c. Robinson projection of the Eastern Hemisphere
    d. Robinson projection of the Western Hemisphere

72. Which of the following countries are separated by a geometric border?

    a. Turkish Cyprus and Greek Cyprus
    b. North Korea and South Korea
    c. France and Spain
    d. England and Ireland

73. During one year in Grassley County, there are 750 births, 350 deaths, 80 immigrations, and 50 emigrations. What is the natural increase rate for this year?

    a. 400
    b. 830
    c. 430
    d. More information is required.

74. Which of the following is *not* one of the world's four major population agglomerations?
    a. North Africa
    b. Eastern North America
    c. South Asia
    d. Europe

75. Which of the following statements concerning choice theory are correct?
    I. Scarcity forces people, including producers, to make choices
    II. Producers make choices and, as a result, face trade-offs
    III. Opportunity cost is one way to measure the cost of a choice
    a. I only
    b. I and II only
    c. II and III only
    d. I, II, and III

76. John Maynard Keynes advocated what?
    a. Supply-side economics
    b. Demand-side economics
    c. Laissez faire economics
    d. The Laffer Curve

77. If a society wants greater income equity, it will:
    a. impose a progressive income tax.
    b. impose high estate taxes.
    c. impose a gift tax.
    d. All of the above

78. Which of the following best defines American GDP?
    a. The value, in American dollars, of all goods and services produced within American borders during one calendar year
    b. The value, in American dollars, of all goods and services produced by American companies during one calendar year
    c. The total value, in American dollars, of all American household incomes during one calendar year
    d. The value, in American dollars, of a "market basket" of goods and services in one year divided by the value of the same market basket in a previous year multiplied by 100

79. Ivy loses her job because her skills as a seamstress are no longer required due to a new piece of machinery that does the work of a seamstress more quickly and for less money. Which type of unemployment is this?
    a. Frictional
    b. Structural
    c. Cyclical
    d. Careless

Mometrix

80. Which is considered part of the natural rate of unemployment?

    I. Structural unemployment
    II. Frictional unemployment
    III. Cyclical unemployment

  a. I only
  b. II only
  c. III only
  d. I and II only

81. Which of the following is a supply shock likely to produce?

    I. An increase in input prices
    II. An increase in price levels
    III. A decrease in employment
    IV. A decrease in GDP

  a. I and III only
  b. II and IV only
  c. I, II, and III only
  d. I, II, III, and IV

82. Which of the following are true of the demand curve?

    I. It is normally downward sloping
    II. It is normally upward sloping
    III. It is influenced by the law of diminishing marginal unity
    IV. It is unaffected by the law of diminishing marginal unity

  a. I and III only
  b. I and IV only
  c. II and III only
  d. II and IV only

83. The price of fleece blankets goes up from $10 to $11. At the same time, demand goes down from 1,000 blankets to 800 blankets. Which of the following statements is true?

  a. Demand is elastic
  b. Demand is inelastic
  c. The price elasticity quotient, or E_d, is less than 1
  d. The price elasticity quotient, or E_d, is equal to 1

84. The price of oil drops dramatically, saving soda pop manufacturers great amounts of money spent on making soda pop and delivering their product to market. Prices for soda pop, however, stay the same. This is an example of what?

  a. Sticky prices
  b. Sticky wages
  c. The multiplier effect
  d. Aggregate expenditure

85. Which of the following will result if two nations use the theory of comparative advantage when making decisions of which goods to produce and trade?

    a. Each nation will make all of their own goods
    b. Both nations will specialize in the production of the same specific goods
    c. Each nation will specialize in the production of different specific goods
    d. Neither nation will trade with one another

86. Which of the following is most likely to benefit from inflation?

    a. A bond investor who owns fixed-rate bonds
    b. A retired widow with no income other than fixed Social Security payments
    c. A person who has taken out a fixed-rate loan
    d. A local bank who has loaned money out at fixed rate

87. What does the data in this table most directly describe?

Inputs	1	2	3	4
Output	20	50	80	100

    a. The Law of Diminishing Marginal Returns
    b. Law of Increasing Opportunity Cost
    c. Law of Demand
    d. Consumer surplus

88. How do banks create money?

    a. By printing it
    b. By taking it out of the Federal Reserve
    c. By loaning it out
    d. By putting it into the Federal Reserve

89. Which of the following correctly states the equation of exchange?

    a. MV = PQ
    b. MP x VQ
    c. MP / VQ
    d. VP = MQ

90. Economics is best defined as the study of what?

    a. Scarcity
    b. Business
    c. Trade
    d. Supply and demand

Constructed Response

1. During the latter half of the 19th century, the United States changed into a more and more mobile society. We see this increased mobility in the settling of the West by people from the eastern part of the United States. For many people, this movement westward would bring new opportunities for economic growth; for others this movement meant conflict and the ending of a way of life.

Discuss two reasons why American settlers moved westward. Describe the effect of the railroads on life in the Western United States. Explain how this westward expansion impacted the lives of Native Americans.

2.

Selected Articles From the Articles of Confederation

Article I.   "The Style of this Confederacy shall be "The United States of America."

Article II.   "Each state retains its sovereignty, freedom and independence, and every power, jurisdiction, and right, which is not by this Confederation expressly delegated to the United States, in Congress assembled."

Article III. "The said States hereby severally enter into a firm league of friendship with each other, for their common defense, the security of their liberties and their mutual and general welfare, binding themselves to assist each other, against all force offered to, or attacks made upon them, or any of them, on account of religion, sovereignty, trade, or any other pretense whatever..."

According to the passage above, what form of government in the United States was established by the Articles of Confederation? Identify two advantages states had under this form of government and describe two reasons this form of government was later replaced by the United States Constitution.

3. A decades-long civil war in China ended in 1949, when a group of communist revolutionaries led by Mao Zedong overthrew Chiang Kai-shek's nationalist government and established the People's Republic of China.

Using your knowledge of world history, write an essay in which you:

- Describe two consequences of the Chinese Revolution of 1949
- Analyze how each of the consequences you have identified influenced the development of world history

Answer Key and Explanations

1. D: Of those countries listed here, the two countries whose respective indigenous populations are not as large as the populations of the other countries are Argentina and Uruguay. Argentina's population is approximately 86.4% of European descent, roughly 8% of mestizo (of mixed European and Amerindian heritage), and an estimated 4% of Arab or East Asian ancestry. Uruguay's population is estimated to be 88% of European descent, 4% of African, and 2% of Asian, with 6% of mestizo ancestry in its rural northwest region. Guatemala and Peru (a) have larger indigenous populations. Guatemala, in Central America, has approximately over 40% of its population as indigenous peoples. Peru, in South America, is estimated to have 45% indigenous peoples and 37% partly indigenous peoples for a total of 82%. Ecuador and Bolivia (b) in South America still have indigenous peoples. The population of Ecuador has an estimated 25% indigenous and 65% partly indigenous peoples, for a total of 90%. Paraguay in South America and Mexico in North America (c) both have sizeable indigenous populations. Paraguay's population is estimated to include 95% partly indigenous peoples. Mexico is estimated to have 30% indigenous and 60% partly indigenous peoples in its population for a total of 90%.

2. A: It is not true that England's defeat of the Spanish Armada in 1588 ended their war with Spain. It did establish England's naval dominance and strengthened England's future colonization of the New World, but the actual war between England and Spain did not end until 1604. It is true that Henry VIII's desire to divorce Catherine of Aragon strengthened English expansionism (b). Catherine was Spanish, and Henry split from the Catholic Church because it prohibited divorce. Henry's rejection of his Spanish wife and his subsequent support of the Protestant movement angered King Philip II of Spain and destroyed the formerly close ties between the two countries. When Elizabeth became Queen of England, she supported the Reformation as a Protestant, which also contributed to English colonization (c). Sir Francis Drake, one of the best known English sea captains during this time period, would attack and plunder Spanish ships that had plundered American Indians (d), adding to the enmity between Spain and England. Queen Elizabeth invested in Drake's voyages and gave him her support in claiming territories for England.

3. B: The Virginia Company of London was based in London, not Massachusetts. It had a charter to colonize American land between the Hudson and Cape Fear rivers (c). The other Virginia Company was the Virginia Company of Plymouth, which was based in the American colony of Plymouth, Massachusetts (a). It had a charter to colonize North America between the Potomac River and the northern boundary of Maine (d).

4. C: Hernando Cortes conquered the Mexican Aztecs in 1519. He had several advantages over the Indians, including horses, armor for his soldiers, and guns. In addition, Cortes' troops unknowingly transmitted smallpox to the Aztecs, which devastated their population as they had no immunity to this foreign illness. Vasco Nunez de Balboa (a) was the first European explorer to view the Pacific Ocean when he crossed the Isthmus of Panama in 1513. Juan Ponce de Leon (b) also visited and claimed Florida in Spain's name in 1513. Cabeza de Vaca (d) was one of only four men out of 400 to return from an expedition led by Panfilio de Narvaez in 1528, and was responsible for spreading the story of the Seven Cities of Cibola (the "cities of gold").

5. B: Peter Zenger was an 18th century journalist in New York who was charged with seditious libel after he published articles critical of New York governor William Cosby. His subsequent acquittal in 1735 established a precedent for American freedom of the press. Options A, C, and D can all be rejected because they do not accurately describe the historical significance of Peter Zenger's trial. Although these options name other important freedoms or rights in American history, these rights

157

or freedoms were not central to Peter Zenger's trial. In particular, note that while answers B, C, and D all list rights contained in the First Amendment to the United States Constitution, only B contains the particular right at issue in the Zenger case.

6. A: The attitudes of American colonists after the 1763 Treaty of Paris ended the French and Indian War were not a direct contributor to the American Revolution. American colonists had a supportive attitude toward Great Britain then, and were proud of the part they played in winning the war. Their good will was not returned by British leaders (b), who looked down on American colonials and sought to increase their imperial power over them. Even in 1761, a sign of Americans' objections to having their liberty curtailed by the British was seen when Boston attorney James Otis argued in court against the Writs of Assistance (c), search warrants to enforce England's mercantilist trade restrictions, as violating the kinds of natural laws espoused during the Enlightenment. Lord George Grenville's aggressive program to defend the North American frontier in the wake of Chief Pontiac's attacks included stricter enforcement of the Navigation Acts, the Proclamation of 1763, the Sugar Act (or Revenue Act), the Currency Act, and most of all the Stamp Act (d). Colonists objected to these as taxation without representation. Other events followed in this taxation dispute, which further eroded Americans' relationship with British government, including the Townshend Acts, the Massachusetts Circular Letter, the Boston Massacre, the Tea Act, and the resulting Boston Tea Party. Finally, with Britain's passage of the Intolerable Acts and the Americans' First Continental Congress, which was followed by Britain's military aggression against American resistance, actual warfare began in 1775. While not all of the colonies wanted war or independence by then, things changed by 1776, and Jefferson's Declaration of Independence was formalized.

7. C: Colonists did find that tea shipped directly by the British East India Company cost less than smuggled Dutch tea, even with tax. The colonists, however, did not buy it. They refused, despite its lower cost, on the principle that the British were taxing colonists without representation (d). It is true that the British East India Company lost money as a result of colonists buying tea smuggled from Holland (a). They sought to remedy this problem by getting concessions from Parliament to ship tea directly to the colonies instead of going through England (b) as the Navigation Acts normally required. Boston Governor Thomas Hutchinson, who sided with Britain, stopped tea ships from leaving the harbor, which after 20 days would cause the tea to be sold at auction. At that time, British taxes on the tea would be paid. On the 19th night after Hutchinson's action, American protestors held the Boston Tea Party, dressing as Indians and dumping all the tea into the harbor to destroy it so it could not be taxed and sold. Many American colonists disagreed with the Boston Tea Party because it involved destroying private property.

8. C: Massachusetts did set a valuable example for other states by stipulating that its constitution should be created via a special convention rather than via the legislature. This way, the constitution would take precedence over the legislature, which would be subject to the rules of the constitution. It is not true that twelve states had new constitutions by the end of 1777 (a). By this time, ten of the states had new constitutions. It is not true that Connecticut and <u>Massachusetts</u> retained their colonial charters minus the British parts (b). Connecticut and <u>Rhode Island</u> were the states that preserved their colonial charters. They simply removed any parts referring to British rule. Massachusetts did not formalize its new constitution in <u>1778</u> (d). This state did not actually finish the process of adopting its new constitution until <u>1780</u>.

9. D: The Louisiana Purchase actually increased the U.S.'s territory by 100% overnight, not 50%. The Louisiana territory doubled the size of the nation. It is true that Jefferson initially sent a delegation to Paris to see if Napoleon would agree to sell only New Orleans to the United States (a). It is also true that Napoleon, who expected America to encroach on Louisiana, decided to avoid this by offering to sell the entire territory to the U.S. (b). It is likewise true that America only had authority to buy New Orleans. Nevertheless, the delegation accepted Napoleon's offer of all of Louisiana (c).

10. B: Hamilton did not object to U.S. western expansionism, and Burr did not support it. There were certain Federalists other than Hamilton who opposed expansion to the west as a threat to their position within the Union, and these opponents did attempt to organize a movement to secede (a). To get Aaron Burr to champion their cause, they offered to help him run for Governor of New York (c). Hamilton did lead the opposition against Burr's campaign (d).

11. A: The U.S. did carry out a three-pronged invasion of Canada early in the war, but they did not succeed on two fronts. Instead, they lost on all three. Americans did win sea battles against the British early in the war, but were soon beaten back to their homeports and then blockaded by powerful British warships (b). Admiral Perry did defeat the British on Lake Erie on September 10, 1813 (c). Perry's victory allowed William Henry Harrison to invade Canada (d) in October of 1813, where he defeated British and Indians in the Battle of the Thames.

12. D: Political corruption was not an immediate effect of the rapid urban growth during this time. The accelerated growth of cities in America did soon result in services being unable to keep up with that growth. The results of this included deficiencies in clean water delivery and garbage collection, causing poor sanitation (a). That poor sanitation led to outbreaks of cholera and typhus, as well as typhoid fever epidemics (b). Police and fire fighting services could not keep up with the population increases, and were often inadequate (c).

13. D: All the laws (d) named were instrumental in spurring westward migration to the Great Plains. The Homestead Act (a), passed in 1862, gave settlers 160 acres of land at no monetary cost in exchange for a commitment to cultivating the land for five years. The Timber Culture Act (b), passed in 1873, gave the settlers 160 acres more of land in exchange for planting trees on one quarter of the acreage. The Desert Land Act (c), passed in 1877, allowed buyers who would irrigate the land to buy 640 acres for only 25 cents an acre. Thus, (d), all of these laws were instrumental in spurring westward migration to the Great Plains during that period, is correct.

14. B: Germany's declaration of war on Russia in 1914, following the assassination of Archduke Ferdinand (b), did not contribute to ending American neutrality in World War I. Once Germany declared war, England, France, Italy, Russia, and Japan joined as the Allied Powers against the Central Powers of Germany and Austria-Hungary, and US President Woodrow Wilson declared America's neutrality. When Germany designated the area surrounding the British Isles as a war zone in February 1913 (a), and warned all ships from neutral countries to stay out of the zone, an end to American neutrality was prompted. President Wilson's responded to Germany's declaration by proclaiming that America would hold Germany responsible for any American losses of life or property. When Germany sank the British passenger vessel *Lusitania*, 128 American passengers were killed (c). This further eroded Wilson's resolve to remain neutral. In February 1917, Germany declared unrestricted submarine warfare on any ship in the war zone (d); this signified that ships from any country would face German attack.

15. A: The postwar conference that brought US-Soviet differences to light was (a) the Potsdam conference in July of 1945. The conference at Yalta (b), in February of 1945, resulted in the division of Germany into Allied-controlled zones. The Dumbarton Oaks conference (c) (1944) established a Security Council, on which with the US, England, Soviet Union, France, and China served as the five permanent members. Each of the permanent members had veto power, and a General Assembly, with limited power, was also established. The Tehran conference (d) included FDR's proposal for a new international organization to take the place of the League of Nations. This idea would later be realized in the form of the United Nations.

16. D: In 1956, Egypt did not attack Israel. On October 29, 1956, Israel attacked Egypt. England and France did join this war within two days. It is true that Egyptian President Gamal Abdul Nasser refused to take America's side in the Cold War (a). In reaction to his refusal, President Eisenhower's administration pulled its funding from the Aswan Dam project in Egypt (b). Nasser then nationalized the British-owned Suez Canal (c).

17. C: The person or group not instrumental in advancing civil rights and desegregation immediately after WWII was (c), Congress. As African American soldiers came home from the war, racial discord increased. President Harry Truman (a) appointed a Presidential Committee on Civil Rights in 1946. This committee published a report recommending that segregation and lynching be outlawed by the federal government. However, Congress ignored this report and took no action. Truman then used his presidential powers to enforce desegregation of the military and policies of "fair employment" in federal civil service jobs. The National Association for the Advancement of Colored People (NAACP) (d) brought lawsuits against racist and discriminatory practices, and in resolving these suits, the Supreme Court (b) further eroded segregation. For example, the Supreme Court ruled that primaries allowing only whites would be illegal, and it ended the segregation of interstate bus lines. The landmark civil rights laws were not passed by Congress until the 1960s.

18. B: Of the programs enacted by Johnson, the one most closely related to JFK's legacy was (b), the Civil Rights Act, which Johnson pushed through Congress using allusions to Kennedy's and his goals. While Kennedy received congressional backing for a raise in minimum wage and public housing improvements, his efforts regarding civil rights were thwarted by conservative Republicans and Southern Democrats in Congress. However, as the Civil Rights movement progressed through the campaigns of the Freedom Riders, Kennedy developed a strong commitment to the cause.

The Economic Opportunity Act gave almost $1 billion to wage Johnson's War on Poverty. The Great Society (c) was Johnson's name for his comprehensive reform program which included a variety of legislation (see also question #102).

19. B: The GATT countries did agree to abolish or decrease many of their tariffs, but this agreement did not include only 57 countries. It was much larger, including a total of 117 countries. The GATT was approved by Congress in 1994 (a). In addition to having 117 countries agree to increase free trade, the GATT also set up the World Trade Organization (WTO) for the purpose of settling any differences among nations related to trade (c). Another instance of free trade policy established in the 1990s was the Senate's ratification of NAFTA. The negotiation of this agreement was originally made by the first Bush administration, with President Bush and the leaders of Canada and Mexico signing it in 1992 (d), but it still needed to be ratified.

20. B: There was not a reduction in military spending after the war. Although the manufacturing demand for war supplies and the size of the military decreased, the government had increased military spending from $10 billion in 1947 to more than $50 billion by 1953—a more than fivefold increase. This increase strengthened the American economy. Other factors contributing to the strengthened economy included the significantly higher birth rates during the Baby Boom (a) from 1946 to 1957, which stimulated the growth of the building and automotive industries by increased demand. Government programs, such as the GI Bill (the Servicemen's Readjustment Act of 1944), other veterans' benefits, and the National Defense Education Act all encouraged college enrollments, which increased by nearly four times (c). Additionally, larger families, increased mobility and low-interest loans offered to veterans led to suburban development and growth (d) as well as an increased home construction.

21. D: The statement that the 1986 Immigration Reform and Control Act reduced illegal Mexican immigration is not true. This legislation punished employers with sanctions for hiring undocumented employees, but despite this the illegal immigration of Mexicans to America was largely unaffected by the law. It is true that twice as many people immigrated to America in the 1980s than in the 1970s (a): the number reached over nine million in the 80s. It is true that the majority of immigrants were Latin American (b). In addition to Latin Americans, other large groups of immigrants in the 1980s were Asians and Caribbean inhabitants (c).

22. C: The Mississippi Freedom Democratic Party did attend the 1964 Democratic convention; however, they were unable garner Johnson's support to unseat the regular delegation from Mississippi. A riot did break out in Watts in 1965 (a), and in the following three years, more riots occurred in Newark, N.J. (b) and in Detroit, Michigan (d). These riots were manifestations of the frustrations experienced by blacks regarding racial inequities in American society.

23. A: The earliest written language in Mesopotamia was Sumerian. Ancient Sumerians began writing this language around 3500 B.C.E. Elamite (b), from Iran, was the language spoken by the ancient Elamites and was the official language of the Persian Empire from the 6th to 4th centuries B.C.E. Written Linear Elamite was used for a very short time in the late 3rd century B.C.E. The written Elamite cuneiform, used from about 2500 to 331 B.C.E., was an adaptation of the Akkadian (c) cuneiform. Akkadian is the earliest found Semitic language. Written Akkadian cuneiform first appeared in texts by circa 2800 B.C.E., and full Akkadian texts appeared by circa 2500 B.C.E. The Akkadian cuneiform writing system is ultimately a derivative of the ancient Sumerian cuneiform writing system, although these two spoken languages were not related linguistically. Aramaic (d) is another Semitic language, but unlike Akkadian, Aramaic is not now extinct. Old Aramaic, the written language of the Old Testament and the spoken language used by Jesus Christ, was current from c. 1100-200 C.E. Middle Aramaic, used from 200-1200 C.E., included literary Syriac (Christian groups developed the writing system of Syriac in order to be able to write spoken Aramaic) and was the written language of the Jewish books of Biblical commentary (Namely, the Talmud, the Targum, and the Midrash). Modern Aramaic has been used from 1200 to the present.

24. C: The New Kingdom was the period during which no more pyramids were built in Egypt. The Pyramids were built between the years of 2630 and 1814 B.C.E., and the New Kingdom spanned from circa 1550-1070 B.C. As a result, the last pyramid was built approximately 264 years before the New Kingdom began. 2630 B.C.E. marked the beginning of the reign of the first Pharaoh, Djoser, who had the first pyramid built at Saqqara. 1814 B.C.E. marked the end of the reign of the last Pharaoh, Amenemhat III, who had the last pyramid built at Hawara. In between these years, a succession of pharaohs built many pyramids. The Old Kingdom (a) encompasses both the Third (d) and Fourth Dynasties; therefore, both choices encompass pyramid-building periods. Djoser's had his first pyramid built during the Third Dynasty (d). The Pharaohs Kufu, Khafre, and Menkaure, respectively, build the famous Pyramids of Giza during the Fourth Dynasty during their reigns at different times between circa 2575 and 2467 B.C.E., the period of the Fourth Dynasty. The Middle Kingdom (b) encompassed the 11th through 14th Dynasties, from circa 2080 to 1640 B.C.E.—also within the time period (2630-1814 B.C.E.) when pyramids were built by the Pharaohs.

25. B: It is not true that the Crusades succeeded at Christians' reclaiming the "holy land" (the Middle East) from Muslims. Despite their number (nine not counting the Northern Crusades) and longevity (1095-1291 not counting later similar campaigns), the Crusades never accomplished this purpose (a). While they did not take back the Middle East, the Crusades did succeed in exacerbating

161

the decline of the Byzantine Empire (c), which lost more and more territory to the Ottoman Turks during this period. In addition, the Crusades resulted in Egypt's rise once again to become a major power (d) of the Middle East as it had been in the past.

26. D: All these events contributed to the Italian Renaissance. After the Black Death killed a third of Europe's population (a), the survivors were mainly upper classes with more money to spend on art, architecture, and other luxuries. The plague deaths also resulted in a labor shortage, thereby creating more work opportunities for the surviving people in lower classes (b). As a result, these survivors' positions in society appreciated. Once plague deaths subsided and population growth in Europe began to reassert itself, a greater demand existed for products and services. At the same time, the number of people available to provide these products and services was still smaller than in the past. Consequently, more merchants, artisans, and bankers emerged in order to provide the services and products people wanted, thereby creating a class of citizens between the lower class laborers and the upper class elite (c).

27. B: In order to prosper, a nation should not try to increase its imports. Mercantilism is an economic theory including the idea that prosperity comes from a positive balance of international trade. For any one nation to prosper, that nation should increase its exports (c) but decrease its imports. Exporting more to other countries while importing less from them will give a country a positive trade balance. This theory assumes that money and wealth are identical (a) assets of a nation. Mercantilism dictates that a nation's government should apply a policy of economic protectionism (d) by stimulating more exports and suppressing imports. Some ways to do accomplish this task have included granting subsidies for exports and imposing tariffs on imports. Mercantilism can be regarded as essentially the opposite of the free trade policies that have been encouraged in more recent years.

28. C: It is not true that the English Civil Wars between 1641 and 1651 legalized Parliament's consent as a requirement for a monarch to rule England. These wars did establish this idea as a precedent, but the later Glorious Revolution of 1688 actually made it legal that a monarch could not rule without Parliamentary consent. The wars from 1641-1651 were all fought between Royalists who supported an absolute monarchy and Parliamentarians who supported the joint government of a parliamentary monarchy (a). Parliament was the victor (b) in 1651 at the Battle of Worcester. As a result of this battle, King Charles I was executed, and King Charles II was exiled. In the first of these civil wars, from 1642-1646, and the second, from 1648-1649, supporters of King Charles I (d) fought against supporters of the Long Parliament.

29. D: Resentment against the Protestant Reformation was not a cause given for the French Revolution. Choices (a), (b), and (c) are just a few among many causes cited for the war. Famines caused malnutrition and even starvation among the poorest people (a). Escalating bread prices contributed greatly to the hunger. Louis XV had amassed a great amount of debt from spending money on many wars in addition to the American Revolution. Military failures as well as a lack of social services for veterans exacerbated these debts. In addition, the Court of Louis XVI and Marie Antoinette spent excessively and obviously on luxuries even while people in the country were starving, and France's monetary system was outdated, inefficient, and thus unable to manage the national debt (b). Much of the populace greatly resented the Catholic Church's control of the country (c). However, there was not great resentment against the Protestant Reformation (d); there were large minorities of Protestants in France, who not only exerted their influence on government institutions, but undoubtedly also contributed to the resentment of the Catholic Church.

30. A: In the 1780s, the French national debt was very high. The French nobility adamantly resisted attempts by King Louis XVI to reform tax laws, which led to a high tax burden on the French peasantry. The French government spent almost 50% of its national expenditures on debt-related payments during the 1780s; thus it could not and did not spend almost 60% to finance luxuries for the French nobility. This eliminates choice B. King Louis XVI temporarily banned the guild system to bolster, rather than stifle, free trade. Because this system gave skilled craftsmen economic advantages, journeymen opposed ending the system. This eliminates choice D. Regardless of the status of guilds before the French Revolution, French society did not offer many opportunities for upward social mobility. Few peasants were able to advance. This eliminates choice C.

31. C: The only accurate statement about the end of WWI is that President Wilson had proposed that the nations of the world form a coalition to prevent future world wars. While he did not give the coalition a name, he clearly expressed his proposal that such a group form in the fourteenth of his Fourteen Points. The Treaty of Versailles (1919) did not bring peace among all countries involved in the war (a); Germany and the United States arrived at a separate peace in 1921. Furthermore, the Treaty of Versailles did not contain a clause for establishing the United Nations (b); it contained a clause for establishing the League of Nations. The League of Nations was created as dictated by the treaty, but when the Second World War proved that this group had failed to prevent future world wars, it was replaced by the United Nations after World War II. President Wilson did not succeed in getting the USA to ratify the League of Nations (d).

32. A: Russian's involvement in World War I brought social tension in Russia to a head. Contributing factors included military defeats and civilian suffering. Prior to Russia entering the war, Russian factory workers could legally strike, but during the war, it was illegal for them to act collectively. This eliminates answer C. Protests continued during World War I, and the Russian government was overthrown in 1917. This eliminates answer D. Answer B can be rejected because World War ___ did not go well for the Russian Army; Nicholas III, therefore, had no successes upon which to capitalize.

33. The last occurring decolonization event was the Eastern Bloc and Soviet Satellite states of ___, Azerbaijan, Estonia, Georgia, Kazakhstan, Kyrgyzstan, Latvia, Lithuania, Moldova, Russia, ___, Turkmenistan, Ukraine, and Uzbekistan all became independent from the Soviet Union in 1991. (Note: This was the last decolonization of the Cold War years, as the end of the Soviet Union marked the end of the Cold War.) Canada completed its independence from British Parliament via the Canada Act (b) in 1982. In the Caribbean, the Bahamas gained independence from the United Kingdom (__ 1973. Algeria won its independence from France when the Algerian War of Independence, begun in 1954, ended in 1962 (d).

34. U.S. industrialization was confined to the Northeast until after the Civil War because the Northeast had faster-running rivers than the South. The earliest American factories used horse-drawn machines. When waterpower was developed and proved superior, the Northeast's faster rivers were more suited to water-powered mills than the South's slower rivers. The war did not delay the development of water power (a). Waterpower was developed before the Civil War in the late 1790s. Steam power, a more efficient alternative to water power, was developed after the Civil War and eventually replaced waterpower. With steam-powered engines, industry could spread to the South, since steam engines did not depend on rapidly running water like water-powered engines. While British emigré Samuel Slater's first cotton mill using horse-drawn production did lose a lot of money (c), this was not a reason for industrial delay. In fact, Slater's Beverly Cotton Manufactory in Massachusetts, the first American cotton mill, in spite of its financial problems, was successful in both its volume of cotton production and in developing the water-powered technology that ultimately would succeed the horse-drawn method. Slater's second cotton mill in Pawtucket, Rhode Island, was water-powered. Industrial delay was not because milling technology had not yet been invented (d). Slater learned of new textile manufacturing techniques as a youth in England,

163

and he brought this knowledge to America in 1789. Resistance of Southern owners of plantations and slaves did not slow the spread of industrialism. Rather, as seen in (b) above, the South did not have the geographic capability to sustain waterpower. Once steam power was developed, the South joined in industrialization.

35. A: The inaccurate statement is the Puritans unconditionally supported the English Reformation. While they agreed with the Reformation in principle, they felt that it had not pursued those principles far enough and should make greater reforms. Similarly, they felt that the Church of England (or Anglican Church), though it had separated from the Catholic Church in the Protestant Reformation, still allowed many practices they found too much like Catholicism (b). The Puritans did become a chief political power in England because of the first English Civil War (c) between Royalists and Parliamentarians. The Royalists had a profound suspicion of the radical Puritans. Among the Parliament's elements of resistance, the strongest was that of the Puritans. They joined in the battle initially for ostensibly political reasons as others had, but soon they brought more attention to religious issues. Following the Restoration in 1660 and the Uniformity Act of 1662, thereby restoring the Church of England to its pre-English Civil War status, the great majority of Puritan clergy defected from the Church of England (d).

36. D: It is not true that the Gilded Age is a term whose origins have not been identified clearly. In 1873, Mark Twain and Charles Dudley Warner co-authored a book entitled The Gilded Age: A Tale of Today. Twain and Warner first coined this term to describe the extravagance and excesses of America's wealthy upper class (b), who became richer than ever due to industrialization. Furthermore, the Gilded Age was the era of the "robber barons" (a) such as John D. Rockefeller, Cornelius Vanderbilt, J.P. Morgan, and others. Because they accumulated enormous wealth through extremely aggressive and occasionally unethical monetary manipulations, critics dubbed them "robber barons" because they seemed to be elite lords of robbery. While these business tycoons grasped huge fortunes, some of them—such as Andrew Carnegie and Andrew Mellon—were also philanthropists, using their wealth to support and further worthy causes such as literacy, education, health care, charities, and the arts. They donated millions of dollars to fund social improvements. Carnegie himself dubbed this large philanthropic movement the "Gospel of Wealth" (c).

37. A: It is not true that the founding fathers specifically stated in the Constitution that the USA would be a democracy. The founding fathers wanted the new United States to be founded on principles of liberty and equality, but they did not specifically describe these principles with the term "Democracy." Thus, the Declaration of Independence, like the Constitution after it, did not stipulate a democracy, although both did state the principles of equality and freedom (b). The Constitution also provided for the election of the new government (c), and for protection of the rights of some, but not all, of the people (d). Notable exceptions at the time were black people and women. Only later were laws passed to protect their rights over the years.

38. B: Preservatives such as salt were only introduced to the European diet after trade routes opened and these goods could be brought to Europe.

39. B: In 1792, when the French Revolution turned into European war, American traders conducted business with both sides. It is not true that Washington allied with the French (a) at this time. Washington issued a Proclamation of Neutrality in 1792 when the French went to war with European countries. While they did trade with both sides, American merchants profited the most from the French West Indies, not the British West Indies (c). The Spanish navy did not retaliate against America for trading with the French (d). Though Spain was an ally of Britain, it was the British who most often seized American ships and forced their crews to serve the British navy.

40. B: The Etruscans were from a kingdom to the north that seized control of Rome from the Latins in the mid-600s B.C. They began urbanizing the settlement, improving roads, adding drainage systems, etc. They were driven out of the region in 509 B.C. during an uprising of the Latins.

41. A: James Madison, John Jay, and Alexander Hamilton published The Federalist in the Independent Journal in New York. It was a response to the Anti-Federalists in New York, who were slow to ratify the Constitution because they feared it gave the central government too much authority.

42. D: A practical application of content learned involves action, not merely knowledge. Options A and C, although they describe content that students would reasonably learn in a class or unit on the structure of the U.S. government, do not describe applications of content, or applications of a social studies education. Therefore options A and C can both be rejected. Option B does involve action and not merely the acquisition of knowledge. However, it is not as directly tied to learning the structure of the U.S. government as option D, informed participation in U.S. political processes. This is because informed participation in school elections is quite possible without knowing the structure of the U.S. government. Informed participation in U.S. political processes requires knowledge of the structure of the U.S. government (i.e., voting on an issue requires an understanding of where a given candidate stands on that issue).

43. C: A federalist system of government is a government under which power is shared by a central authority and sub-components of the federation. In the United States in particular, power is shared by the federal government and the individual states. Option A, that the legislative branch consists of two representative bodies (the House of Representatives and the Senate) is true, of course, but does not describe a uniquely federalist structure. Rather, it describes the concept of bicameralism. Option A may thus be eliminated. Option B, likewise, describes different types of democracy but not federalism. B can thus be eliminated. Regarding option D, this statement is also true (the U.S. Constitution shapes national legislation) but it is not a descriptive statement of the federalist system because the statement makes no mention that power is shared by the states.

44. D: Congress did not have the authority to levy taxes under the Articles of Confederation. Without the ability to levy taxes, there was no way to finance programs, which weakened the government.

45. A: The Age of Enlightenment was a time of scientific and philosophical achievement. Also called the Age of Reason, human thought and reason were prized.

46. C: The Constitution was not ratified immediately. Only five states accepted it in early 1788; Massachusetts, New York, Rhode Island, and Virginia were originally opposed to the Constitution. Rhode Island reluctantly accepted it in 1790.

47. B: James Madison was a close friend of Thomas Jefferson and supported a stronger central government. George Mason and Robert Yates were both against expanding federal authority over the states. Benjamin Franklin was a proponent of a strong federal government, but he was from Massachusetts.

48. D: Some of the men who helped frame the Constitution believed the central government needed to be stronger than what was established under the Articles of Confederation. Others were against this and feared a strong federal government. A system of checks and balances was established to prevent the central government from taking too much power. This arrangement is known as federalism.

49. A: The Senate and House of Representatives make up a bicameral legislature. The Great Compromise awarded seats in the Senate equally to each state, while the seats in the House of Representatives were based on population.

50. B: The Presidential Succession Act lists the Speaker of the House, President Pro Tempore of the Senate, and Secretary of State next in succession after the Vice President. However, anyone who succeeds as President must meet all of the legal qualifications.

51. C: The President has the power to veto legislation directly or use a pocket veto by not signing a bill within ten days after receiving it. Congress adjourns during this time period. A veto can be overridden if two-thirds of the House and the two-thirds of the Senate both agree. The President must veto a complete bill and does not have the authority to veto sections or lines.

52. C: The Civil Rights Act of 1964 affected the Jim Crow laws in the Southern states. Many minorities suffered under unfair voting laws and segregation. President Lyndon Johnson signed the Civil Rights Act of 1964 into law after the 1963 assassination of President Kennedy, who championed the reform.

53. B: Only the federal government has the power to give copyrights and patents to individuals or companies. The power to levy taxes, borrow money, and spend money (a) is a power shared by federal and state governments. The power to set the criteria that qualify individuals to vote (c) is a power given to state governments only. The power to ratify amendments proposed to the Constitution (d) is a power of only the state governments.

54. A: The action that needs a three-fourths majority vote is state approval of a proposed constitutional amendment. Proposing a constitutional amendment (b) requires a two-thirds majority vote. Ratifying presidential appointments in the Senate (c) also requires a two-thirds majority vote. Introducing charges for impeachment in the House of Representatives (d) requires a simple majority vote.

55. B: The term "Manifest Destiny" had not been used for many years before the 1830s. This term was coined in 1844. However, it is true that the idea this term expressed had been around for many years before that (a). It is also true that many Americans believed Manifest Destiny would mean America would ultimately encompass Canada and Mexico (c). Factors contributing to Manifest Destiny included the rise in nationalism that followed the War of 1812 and the population growth that increased that nationalism (d).

56. A: Presidential candidates are eligible for a match from the federal government (with a $250 per contribution limit) if they can privately raise $5,000 per state in twenty states. Candidates who accept public money agree to limit spending. Candidates who do not accept matching funds are free to use the money they raise privately.

57. D: America is a common law country because English common law was adopted in all states except Louisiana. Common law is based on precedent, and changes over time. Each state develops its own common laws.

58. D: The only answer choice that represents a possible absolute location for New Orleans is 30° N, 90° W. When a location is described in terms of its placement on the global grid, it is customary to put the latitude before the longitude. New Orleans is north of the equator, so it has to be in the Northern Hemisphere. In addition, it is west of the prime meridian, which runs through Greenwich, England, among other places. So, New Orleans must be in the Western Hemisphere. It is possible, then, to deduce that 30° N, 90° W is the only possible absolute location for New Orleans.

59. B: On a political map, countries are represented in different colors, and countries that share a border are not given the same color. This is so that the borders between countries will be distinct. Political maps are used to illustrate those aspects of a country that have been determined by people: the capital, the provincial and national borders, and the large cities. Political maps sometimes include major physical features like rivers and mountains, but they are not intended to display all such information. On a physical, climate, or contour map, however, the borders between nations are more incidental. Colors are used on these maps to represent physical features, areas with similar climate, etc. It is possible that colors will overrun the borders and be shared by adjacent countries.

60. D: Around the world, the area around the equator is known for a relative lack of wind. Indeed, the equatorial belt is sometimes called the doldrums because the constant warm water encourages the air to rise gently. To the north and south, however, there are trade winds that can become quite violent. The equator only intersects three continents: Asia, Africa, and South America. It is in between the north and south horse latitudes, which are belts known for calm winds. Finally, the equator is located at 0° latitude, not longitude, though the 0° line of longitude does intersect the equator.

61. A: The apparent distance between Greenland and Norway will be greatest on a Mercator map. The Mercator map is a type of cylindrical projection map in which lines of latitude and longitude are transferred onto a cylindrical shape, which is then cut vertically and laid flat. For this reason, distances around the poles will appear increasingly great. The Mercator map is excellent for navigation because a straight line drawn on it represents a single compass reading. In a conic projection map, on the other hand, a hemisphere of the globe is transposed onto a cone, which is then cut vertically (that is, from rim to tip) and laid flat. The apparent distances on a conic projection will be smallest at the 45th parallel. A contour map uses lines to illustrate the features of a geographic area. For example, the lines on an elevation contour map connect areas that have the same altitude. An equal-area projection map represents landmasses in their actual sizes. To make this possible, the shapes of the landmasses are manipulated slightly, and the map is interrupted (divided into more than one part).

62. A: Symbols are not used to represent relief on a physical map. A physical map is dedicated to illustrating the landmasses and bodies of water in a specific region, so symbols do not provide enough detail. Color, shading, and contour lines, on the other hand, are able to create a much more complicated picture of changes in elevation, precipitation, etc. Changes in elevation are known in geography as relief.

63. D: A flow-line map describes the movement of people, trends, or materials across a physical area. The movements depicted on a flow-line map are typically represented by arrows. In more advanced flow-line maps, the width of the arrow corresponds to the quantity of the motion. Flow-line maps usually declare the span of time that is being represented. A political map depicts the man-made aspects of geography, such as borders and cities. A cartogram adjusts the size of the areas represented according to some variable. For instance, a cartogram of wheat production would depict Iowa as being much larger than Alaska. A qualitative map uses lines, dots, and other symbols to illustrate a particular point. For example, a qualitative map might be used to demonstrate the greatest expansion of the Persian Empire.

64. B: The composite volcano, sometimes called the stratovolcano, is the most common type of volcano on earth. A composite volcano has steep sides, so the explosions of ash, pumice, and silica are often accompanied by treacherous mudslides. Indeed, it is these mudslides that cause most of the damage associated with composite volcano eruptions. Krakatoa and Mount Saint Helens are examples of composite volcanoes. A lava dome is a round volcano that emits thick lava very slowly. A shield volcano, one example of which is Mt. Kilauea in Hawaii, emits a small amount of lava over an extended period of time. Shield volcanoes are not known for violent eruptions. A cinder cone has steep sides made of fallen cinders, which themselves are made of the lava that intermittently shoots into the air.

65. C: After precipitation, the heat of the sun causes evaporation, a process by which water molecules change from a liquid to a gas, ultimately returning to the atmosphere. The other options describe processes that pertain to properties of water, but not to water's return to the atmosphere. Percolation is the process by which water moves down through soil. Cohesion (specifically, structural cohesion) is the property of matter by which the molecules in a single substance stay together. Condensation is the process by which matter changes from a gas to a liquid; after evaporation, molecules of water form rain droplets through condensation.

66. B: Metamorphic rock is formed by extreme heat and pressure. This type of rock is created when other rocks are somehow buried within the earth, where they are subject to a dramatic rise in pressure and temperature. Slate and marble are both metamorphic rocks. Metamorphic rocks are created by the other two main types of rock: sedimentary and igneous. Sedimentary rock is formed when dirt and other sediment is washed into a bed, covered over by subsequent sediment, and compacted into rock. Depending on how they are formed, sedimentary rocks are classified as organic, clastic, or chemical. Igneous rocks are composed of cooled magma, the molten rock that emerges from volcanoes. Basalt and granite are two common varieties of igneous rock.

67. A: The eye wall of a hurricane has the strongest winds and the greatest rainfall. The eye wall is the tower-like rim of the eye. It is from this wall that clouds extend out, which are seen from above as the classic outward spiral pattern. A hurricane front is the outermost edge of its influence; although there will be heavy winds and rain in this area, the intensity will be relatively small. The eye of a hurricane is actually a place of surprising peace. In this area, dry and cool air rushes down to the ground or sea. Once there, the air is caught up in the winds of the eye wall and is driven outward at a furious pace.

68. D: These are all geographically parts of Southeast Asia. The countries of Myanmar (Burma), Laos, Cambodia, and Thailand (a) are considered Mainland Southeast Asia, as are Vietnam and the Malay Peninsula (b). Brunei (b), East Malaysia, Indonesia, and the Philippines (c) are considered Maritime Southeast Asia, as are Singapore and Timor-Leste. The Seven Sister States of India are also considered to be part of Southeast Asia, geographically and culturally. (The Seven Sister States of India are Arunachal Pradesh, Assam, Nagaland, Meghalaya, Manipur, Tripura, and Mizoram, which all have contiguous borders in northeastern India.)

69. A: One example of the multiplier effect of large cities would be if the presence of specialized equipment for an industry attracted even more business. Large cities tend to grow even larger for a number of reasons: they have more skilled workers, they have greater concentrations of specialized equipment, and they have already-functioning markets. These factors all make it easier for a business to begin operations in a large city than elsewhere. Thus, the populations and economic productivity of large cities tend to grow quickly. Some governments have sought to mitigate this trend by clustering groups of similar industries in smaller cities.

70. D: The Sahel, a belt of grasslands just south of the Sahara Desert, has long been a focus of agricultural efforts in Africa. This semiarid region has provided sustenance to people and animals for thousands of years. In the last thousand years, stores of salt and gold were found there, giving rise to empires in Ghana and Mali. Changes in climate have expanded the Sahara, however, and pushed the Sahel farther south. The Qattara Depression is a low-lying desert in Egypt. The Great Rift Valley is a region of faults and rocky hills that extends along the southeastern coast of Africa. The Congo Basin is a repository of sediment from the Ubangi and Congo rivers. It is in the northern half of what is now called the Democratic Republic of the Congo.

71. B: To determine the shortest route between Lima and Lisbon, Tracy should use an azimuthal projection with Lisbon at the center. An azimuthal projection depicts one hemisphere of the globe as a circle. A straight line drawn from the center of the map to any point represents the shortest possible distance between those two points. Tracy could obtain her objective, then, with an azimuthal projection in which either Lisbon or Lima were at the center. If the North Pole were at the center, the map would not include Lima because this city is in the Southern Hemisphere. A Robinson projection approximates the sizes and shapes of landmasses but does distort in some ways, particularly near the poles.

72. B: North Korea and South Korea are separated by a geometric border, meaning that the boundary between the two nations is a straight line drawn on a map, without respect to landforms. Specifically, the boundary between the Koreas is the 38th parallel. Another example of a geometric border lies between the continental United States and Canada. The Turkish Cyprus–Greek Cyprus border is anthropogeographic, or drawn according to cultural reasons. The border between France and Spain is physiographic-political, a combination of the Pyrenees Mountains and European history. The Irish Sea separates England from Ireland.

73. D: More information is required to calculate the natural increase rate for Grassley County during this year. Natural increase rate is the growth in population measured as the surplus of live births over deaths for every thousand people. The calculation of natural increase rate does not take account of immigration or emigration. The natural increase rate for Grassley County cannot be calculated because the original population of the county is not given. As an example, if the beginning population of the county had been 10,000, the natural increase rate would be 40; 400 * 1,000/10,000 = 40.

74. A: North Africa is not one of the world's four major population agglomerations. These are eastern North America, South Asia, East Asia, and Europe. The largest of these is East Asia, which encompasses Korea, Japan, and the major cities of China. The second-largest population agglomeration is South Asia, which includes India and Pakistan. Most of the population in this area is near the coasts. The European agglomeration is spread across the largest piece of land, while the much smaller agglomeration in eastern North America is primarily focused on the string of cities from Boston to Washington, DC.

75. D: It is true that scarcity causes producers (and other people) to make choices. Producers must choose what to produce with limited resources. It is also true that the choices a producer makes when faced with scarcity come with trade-offs. There are advantages and disadvantages to different production decisions. And, finally, calculating the opportunity cost of a choice provides a manner with which to measure the consequence of a choice and compare that against the consequence of other choices.

76. B: John Maynard Keynes argued that government could help revitalize a recessionary economy by increasing government spending and therefore increasing aggregate demand. This is known as demand-side economics.

77. D: If a society wants greater income equity, it will impose a progressive income tax, which taxes the wealthy at a higher rate; an inheritance tax, which prevents the wealthy from passing all their wealth on to the next generation; and a gift tax, which prevents the wealthy from simply giving their wealth away.

78. A: Answer B is a definition of gross national product, and answers C and D define other economic measures.

79. B: Structural unemployment is unemployment that results from a mismatch of job skills or location. In this case, Ivy's job skill—her ability to work as a seamstress—is no longer desired by employers. Frictional and cyclical are other forms of unemployment; economists do not use the term careless unemployment.

80. D: It is believed that some level of frictional and structural unemployment will always exist, and that the best economists (and politicians) can hope for is to reduce cyclical unemployment to zero. Therefore, frictional and structural unemployment are sometimes referred to as natural unemployment, meaning unemployment that naturally exists within an economy.

81. D: A supply shock is caused when there is a dramatic increase in input prices. This causes an increase in price levels and decreases in employment and GDP. A supply shock causes the AS curve to move to the left (in).

82. A: As people have more and more of something, they value it less and less. This is the law of diminishing marginal utility, and it is what causes the downward slope of the demand curve.

83. A: The change in demand is 20% (1,000 – 800 = 200), and the change in price is 10% ($11 - $10 = $1). Because the change in demand is greater than the change in price, the demand is considered elastic. In this case, the price elasticity quotient is greater than 1.

84. A: The phenomenon of "sticky prices" refers to prices that stay the same even though it seems they should change (either increasing or decreasing).

85. C: When a nation follows the theory of comparative advantage, it specializes in producing the goods and services it can make at a lower opportunity cost and then engages in trade to obtain other goods.

86. C: A person who has taken out a fixed-rate loan can benefit from inflation by paying back the loan with dollars that are less valuable than they were when the loan was taken out. In the other examples, inflation harms the individual or entity.

87. A: The input and output data illustrates the Law of Diminishing Marginal Returns, which states that as inputs are added during production, there eventually comes a time when increased inputs coincide with a decrease in marginal return.

88. C: Banks create money by giving out loans. For example, assume a person puts $100 into a bank. The bank will keep a percentage of that money in reserves because of the reserve requirement. If the reserve requirement is 10% then the bank will put $10 in reserves and then loan out $90 of it to a second person. The money total, which started at $100, now includes the original $100 plus the $90, or a total of $190. The bank creates $90 by loaning it.

89. A: The equation of exchange is MV = PQ. This means that M1 (a measure of the supply of money) multiplied by the velocity of money (the average number of times a typical dollar is spent on final goods and services a year) = the average price level of final goods and services in GDP x real output, or the quantity of goods and services in GDP.

90. A: Economics is defined as the study of scarcity, the situation in which resources are limited and wants are unlimited.

How to Overcome Test Anxiety

Just the thought of taking a test is enough to make most people a little nervous. A test is an important event that can have a long-term impact on your future, so it's important to take it seriously and it's natural to feel anxious about performing well. But just because anxiety is normal, that doesn't mean that it's helpful in test taking, or that you should simply accept it as part of your life. Anxiety can have a variety of effects. These effects can be mild, like making you feel slightly nervous, or severe, like blocking your ability to focus or remember even a simple detail.

If you experience test anxiety—whether severe or mild—it's important to know how to beat it. To discover this, first you need to understand what causes test anxiety.

Causes of Test Anxiety

While we often think of anxiety as an uncontrollable emotional state, it can actually be caused by simple, practical things. One of the most common causes of test anxiety is that a person does not feel adequately prepared for their test. This feeling can be the result of many different issues such as poor study habits or lack of organization, but the most common culprit is time management. Starting to study too late, failing to organize your study time to cover all of the material, or being distracted while you study will mean that you're not well prepared for the test. This may lead to cramming the night before, which will cause you to be physically and mentally exhausted for the test. Poor time management also contributes to feelings of stress, fear, and hopelessness as you realize you are not well prepared but don't know what to do about it.

Other times, test anxiety is not related to your preparation for the test but comes from unresolved fear. This may be a past failure on a test, or poor performance on tests in general. It may come from comparing yourself to others who seem to be performing better or from the stress of living up to expectations. Anxiety may be driven by fears of the future—how failure on this test would affect your educational and career goals. These fears are often completely irrational, but they can still negatively impact your test performance.

> **Review Video: <u>3 Reasons You Have Test Anxiety</u>**
> Visit mometrix.com/academy and enter code: 428468

Elements of Test Anxiety

As mentioned earlier, test anxiety is considered to be an emotional state, but it has physical and mental components as well. Sometimes you may not even realize that you are suffering from test anxiety until you notice the physical symptoms. These can include trembling hands, rapid heartbeat, sweating, nausea, and tense muscles. Extreme anxiety may lead to fainting or vomiting. Obviously, any of these symptoms can have a negative impact on testing. It is important to recognize them as soon as they begin to occur so that you can address the problem before it damages your performance.

> **Review Video: 3 Ways to Tell You Have Test Anxiety**
> Visit mometrix.com/academy and enter code: 927847

The mental components of test anxiety include trouble focusing and inability to remember learned information. During a test, your mind is on high alert, which can help you recall information and stay focused for an extended period of time. However, anxiety interferes with your mind's natural processes, causing you to blank out, even on the questions you know well. The strain of testing during anxiety makes it difficult to stay focused, especially on a test that may take several hours. Extreme anxiety can take a huge mental toll, making it difficult not only to recall test information but even to understand the test questions or pull your thoughts together.

> **Review Video: How Test Anxiety Affects Memory**
> Visit mometrix.com/academy and enter code: 609003

Effects of Test Anxiety

Test anxiety is like a disease—if left untreated, it will get progressively worse. Anxiety leads to poor performance, and this reinforces the feelings of fear and failure, which in turn lead to poor performances on subsequent tests. It can grow from a mild nervousness to a crippling condition. If allowed to progress, test anxiety can have a big impact on your schooling, and consequently on your future.

Test anxiety can spread to other parts of your life. Anxiety on tests can become anxiety in any stressful situation, and blanking on a test can turn into panicking in a job situation. But fortunately, you don't have to let anxiety rule your testing and determine your grades. There are a number of relatively simple steps you can take to move past anxiety and function normally on a test and in the rest of life.

> **Review Video: How Test Anxiety Impacts Your Grades**
> Visit mometrix.com/academy and enter code: 939819

Mometrix

Physical Steps for Beating Test Anxiety

While test anxiety is a serious problem, the good news is that it can be overcome. It doesn't have to control your ability to think and remember information. While it may take time, you can begin taking steps today to beat anxiety.

Just as your first hint that you may be struggling with anxiety comes from the physical symptoms, the first step to treating it is also physical. Rest is crucial for having a clear, strong mind. If you are tired, it is much easier to give in to anxiety. But if you establish good sleep habits, your body and mind will be ready to perform optimally, without the strain of exhaustion. Additionally, sleeping well helps you to retain information better, so you're more likely to recall the answers when you see the test questions.

Getting good sleep means more than going to bed on time. It's important to allow your brain time to relax. Take study breaks from time to time so it doesn't get overworked, and don't study right before bed. Take time to rest your mind before trying to rest your body, or you may find it difficult to fall asleep.

> **Review Video: The Importance of Sleep for Your Brain**
> Visit mometrix.com/academy and enter code: 319338

Along with sleep, other aspects of physical health are important in preparing for a test. Good nutrition is vital for good brain function. Sugary foods and drinks may give a burst of energy but this burst is followed by a crash, both physically and emotionally. Instead, fuel your body with protein and vitamin-rich foods.

Also, drink plenty of water. Dehydration can lead to headaches and exhaustion, especially if your brain is already under stress from the rigors of the test. Particularly if your test is a long one, drink water during the breaks. And if possible, take an energy-boosting snack to eat between sections.

> **Review Video: How Diet Can Affect your Mood**
> Visit mometrix.com/academy and enter code: 624317

Along with sleep and diet, a third important part of physical health is exercise. Maintaining a steady workout schedule is helpful, but even taking 5-minute study breaks to walk can help get your blood pumping faster and clear your head. Exercise also releases endorphins, which contribute to a positive feeling and can help combat test anxiety.

When you nurture your physical health, you are also contributing to your mental health. If your body is healthy, your mind is much more likely to be healthy as well. So take time to rest, nourish your body with healthy food and water, and get moving as much as possible. Taking these physical steps will make you stronger and more able to take the mental steps necessary to overcome test anxiety.

> **Review Video: How to Stay Healthy and Prevent Test Anxiety**
> Visit mometrix.com/academy and enter code: 877894

Mental Steps for Beating Test Anxiety

Working on the mental side of test anxiety can be more challenging, but as with the physical side, there are clear steps you can take to overcome it. As mentioned earlier, test anxiety often stems from lack of preparation, so the obvious solution is to prepare for the test. Effective studying may be the most important weapon you have for beating test anxiety, but you can and should employ several other mental tools to combat fear.

First, boost your confidence by reminding yourself of past success—tests or projects that you aced. If you're putting as much effort into preparing for this test as you did for those, there's no reason you should expect to fail here. Work hard to prepare; then trust your preparation.

Second, surround yourself with encouraging people. It can be helpful to find a study group, but be sure that the people you're around will encourage a positive attitude. If you spend time with others who are anxious or cynical, this will only contribute to your own anxiety. Look for others who are motivated to study hard from a desire to succeed, not from a fear of failure.

Third, reward yourself. A test is physically and mentally tiring, even without anxiety, and it can be helpful to have something to look forward to. Plan an activity following the test, regardless of the outcome, such as going to a movie or getting ice cream.

When you are taking the test, if you find yourself beginning to feel anxious, remind yourself that you know the material. Visualize successfully completing the test. Then take a few deep, relaxing breaths and return to it. Work through the questions carefully but with confidence, knowing that you are capable of succeeding.

Developing a healthy mental approach to test taking will also aid in other areas of life. Test anxiety affects more than just the actual test—it can be damaging to your mental health and even contribute to depression. It's important to beat test anxiety before it becomes a problem for more than testing.

> **Review Video: <u>Test Anxiety and Depression</u>**
> Visit mometrix.com/academy and enter code: 904704

Study Strategy

Being prepared for the test is necessary to combat anxiety, but what does being prepared look like? You may study for hours on end and still not feel prepared. What you need is a strategy for test prep. The next few pages outline our recommended steps to help you plan out and conquer the challenge of preparation.

Step 1: Scope Out the Test

Learn everything you can about the format (multiple choice, essay, etc.) and what will be on the test. Gather any study materials, course outlines, or sample exams that may be available. Not only will this help you to prepare, but knowing what to expect can help to alleviate test anxiety.

Step 2: Map Out the Material

Look through the textbook or study guide and make note of how many chapters or sections it has. Then divide these over the time you have. For example, if a book has 15 chapters and you have five days to study, you need to cover three chapters each day. Even better, if you have the time, leave an extra day at the end for overall review after you have gone through the material in depth.

If time is limited, you may need to prioritize the material. Look through it and make note of which sections you think you already have a good grasp on, and which need review. While you are studying, skim quickly through the familiar sections and take more time on the challenging parts. Write out your plan so you don't get lost as you go. Having a written plan also helps you feel more in control of the study, so anxiety is less likely to arise from feeling overwhelmed at the amount to cover. A sample plan may look like this:

- Day 1: Skim chapters 1–4, study chapter 5 (especially pages 31–33)
- Day 2: Study chapters 6–7, skim chapters 8–9
- Day 3: Skim chapter 10, study chapters 11–12 (especially pages 87–90)
- Day 4: Study chapters 13–15
- Day 5: Overall review (focus most on chapters 5, 6, and 12), take practice test

Step 3: Gather Your Tools

Decide what study method works best for you. Do you prefer to highlight in the book as you study and then go back over the highlighted portions? Or do you type out notes of the important information? Or is it helpful to make flashcards that you can carry with you? Assemble the pens, index cards, highlighters, post-it notes, and any other materials you may need so you won't be distracted by getting up to find things while you study.

If you're having a hard time retaining the information or organizing your notes, experiment with different methods. For example, try color-coding by subject with colored pens, highlighters, or post-it notes. If you learn better by hearing, try recording yourself reading your notes so you can listen while in the car, working out, or simply sitting at your desk. Ask a friend to quiz you from your flashcards, or try teaching someone the material to solidify it in your mind.

Step 4: Create Your Environment

It's important to avoid distractions while you study. This includes both the obvious distractions like visitors and the subtle distractions like an uncomfortable chair (or a too-comfortable couch that makes you want to fall asleep). Set up the best study environment possible: good lighting and a comfortable work area. If background music helps you focus, you may want to turn it on, but otherwise keep the room quiet. If you are using a computer to take notes, be sure you don't have any other windows open, especially applications like social media, games, or anything else that could distract you. Silence your phone and turn off notifications. Be sure to keep water close by so you stay hydrated while you study (but avoid unhealthy drinks and snacks).

Also, take into account the best time of day to study. Are you freshest first thing in the morning? Try to set aside some time then to work through the material. Is your mind clearer in the afternoon or evening? Schedule your study session then. Another method is to study at the same time of day that you will take the test, so that your brain gets used to working on the material at that time and will be ready to focus at test time.

Step 5: Study!

Once you have done all the study preparation, it's time to settle into the actual studying. Sit down, take a few moments to settle your mind so you can focus, and begin to follow your study plan. Don't give in to distractions or let yourself procrastinate. This is your time to prepare so you'll be ready to fearlessly approach the test. Make the most of the time and stay focused.

Of course, you don't want to burn out. If you study too long you may find that you're not retaining the information very well. Take regular study breaks. For example, taking five minutes out of every hour to walk briskly, breathing deeply and swinging your arms, can help your mind stay fresh.

As you get to the end of each chapter or section, it's a good idea to do a quick review. Remind yourself of what you learned and work on any difficult parts. When you feel that you've mastered the material, move on to the next part. At the end of your study session, briefly skim through your notes again.

But while review is helpful, cramming last minute is NOT. If at all possible, work ahead so that you won't need to fit all your study into the last day. Cramming overloads your brain with more information than it can process and retain, and your tired mind may struggle to recall even previously learned information when it is overwhelmed with last-minute study. Also, the urgent nature of cramming and the stress placed on your brain contribute to anxiety. You'll be more likely to go to the test feeling unprepared and having trouble thinking clearly.

So don't cram, and don't stay up late before the test, even just to review your notes at a leisurely pace. Your brain needs rest more than it needs to go over the information again. In fact, plan to finish your studies by noon or early afternoon the day before the test. Give your brain the rest of the day to relax or focus on other things, and get a good night's sleep. Then you will be fresh for the test and better able to recall what you've studied.

Step 6: Take a practice test

Many courses offer sample tests, either online or in the study materials. This is an excellent resource to check whether you have mastered the material, as well as to prepare for the test format and environment.

Check the test format ahead of time: the number of questions, the type (multiple choice, free response, etc.), and the time limit. Then create a plan for working through them. For example, if you have 30 minutes to take a 60-question test, your limit is 30 seconds per question. Spend less time on the questions you know well so that you can take more time on the difficult ones.

If you have time to take several practice tests, take the first one open book, with no time limit. Work through the questions at your own pace and make sure you fully understand them. Gradually work up to taking a test under test conditions: sit at a desk with all study materials put away and set a timer. Pace yourself to make sure you finish the test with time to spare and go back to check your answers if you have time.

After each test, check your answers. On the questions you missed, be sure you understand why you missed them. Did you misread the question (tests can use tricky wording)? Did you forget the information? Or was it something you hadn't learned? Go back and study any shaky areas that the practice tests reveal.

Taking these tests not only helps with your grade, but also aids in combating test anxiety. If you're already used to the test conditions, you're less likely to worry about it, and working through tests until you're scoring well gives you a confidence boost. Go through the practice tests until you feel comfortable, and then you can go into the test knowing that you're ready for it.

Test Tips

On test day, you should be confident, knowing that you've prepared well and are ready to answer the questions. But aside from preparation, there are several test day strategies you can employ to maximize your performance.

First, as stated before, get a good night's sleep the night before the test (and for several nights before that, if possible). Go into the test with a fresh, alert mind rather than staying up late to study.

Try not to change too much about your normal routine on the day of the test. It's important to eat a nutritious breakfast, but if you normally don't eat breakfast at all, consider eating just a protein bar. If you're a coffee drinker, go ahead and have your normal coffee. Just make sure you time it so that the caffeine doesn't wear off right in the middle of your test. Avoid sugary beverages, and drink enough water to stay hydrated but not so much that you need a restroom break 10 minutes into the test. If your test isn't first thing in the morning, consider going for a walk or doing a light workout before the test to get your blood flowing.

Allow yourself enough time to get ready, and leave for the test with plenty of time to spare so you won't have the anxiety of scrambling to arrive in time. Another reason to be early is to select a good seat. It's helpful to sit away from doors and windows, which can be distracting. Find a good seat, get out your supplies, and settle your mind before the test begins.

When the test begins, start by going over the instructions carefully, even if you already know what to expect. Make sure you avoid any careless mistakes by following the directions.

Then begin working through the questions, pacing yourself as you've practiced. If you're not sure on an answer, don't spend too much time on it, and don't let it shake your confidence. Either skip it and come back later, or eliminate as many wrong answers as possible and guess among the remaining ones. Don't dwell on these questions as you continue—put them out of your mind and focus on what lies ahead.

Be sure to read all of the answer choices, even if you're sure the first one is the right answer. Sometimes you'll find a better one if you keep reading. But don't second-guess yourself if you do immediately know the answer. Your gut instinct is usually right. Don't let test anxiety rob you of the information you know.

If you have time at the end of the test (and if the test format allows), go back and review your answers. Be cautious about changing any, since your first instinct tends to be correct, but make sure you didn't misread any of the questions or accidentally mark the wrong answer choice. Look over any you skipped and make an educated guess.

At the end, leave the test feeling confident. You've done your best, so don't waste time worrying about your performance or wishing you could change anything. Instead, celebrate the successful completion of this test. And finally, use this test to learn how to deal with anxiety even better next time.

> **Review Video: 5 Tips to Beat Test Anxiety**
> Visit mometrix.com/academy and enter code: 570656

Important Qualification

Not all anxiety is created equal. If your test anxiety is causing major issues in your life beyond the classroom or testing center, or if you are experiencing troubling physical symptoms related to your anxiety, it may be a sign of a serious physiological or psychological condition. If this sounds like your situation, we strongly encourage you to seek professional help.

Thank You

We at Mometrix would like to extend our heartfelt thanks to you, our friend and patron, for allowing us to play a part in your journey. It is a privilege to serve people from all walks of life who are unified in their commitment to building the best future they can for themselves.

The preparation you devote to these important testing milestones may be the most valuable educational opportunity you have for making a real difference in your life. We encourage you to put your heart into it—that feeling of succeeding, overcoming, and yes, conquering will be well worth the hours you've invested.

We want to hear your story, your struggles and your successes, and if you see any opportunities for us to improve our materials so we can help others even more effectively in the future, please share that with us as well. **The team at Mometrix would be absolutely thrilled to hear from you!** So please, send us an email (support@mometrix.com) and let's stay in touch.

If you'd like some additional help, check out these other resources we offer for your exam:

http://mometrixflashcards.com/WEST

Additional Bonus Material

Due to our efforts to try to keep this book to a manageable length, we've created a link that will give you access to all of your additional bonus material.

Please visit https://www.mometrix.com/bonus948/westemlhum52 to access the information.